The Collector's Tchaikovsky
and The Five

Keystone Books in Music

THE COLLECTOR'S BACH
by Nathan Broder

THE COLLECTOR'S HAYDN
by C. G. Burke

THE COLLECTOR'S CHOPIN AND SCHUMANN
by Harold C. Schonberg

THE COLLECTOR'S JAZZ
Traditional and Swing
by John S. Wilson

THE COLLECTOR'S JAZZ
Modern
by John S. Wilson

THE COLLECTOR'S TCHAIKOVSKY
AND THE FIVE
by John Briggs

IN PREPARATION

THE COLLECTOR'S TWENTIETH
CENTURY MUSIC
by Arthur Cohn

THE COLLECTOR'S VERDI AND PUCCINI
by Max de Schauensee

THE COLLECTOR'S
TCHAIKOVSKY
AND
THE FIVE

by John Briggs

J. B. LIPPINCOTT COMPANY
Philadelphia & New York

To

MARY CURTIS ZIMBALIST

founder and president
The Curtis Institute of Music
this book is affectionately dedicated
by
a proud wearer
of the old school tie

Contents

TCHAIKOVSKY

THE FIVE

Contents

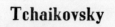

Tchaikovsky

PETER ILYICH TCHAIKOVSKY

Biographical Sketch

FEW MUSCOVITES of 1876 had access to the mansion on the Boulevard Rojdestvensky which was the home of Moscow's richest woman: Nadejda Filaretovna, widow of the railway magnate Karl George Otto von Meck.

Since her husband's death Mme von Meck had lived the life of a recluse. Occasionally she went to a symphony concert, sitting determinedly incognito in the balcony. Otherwise she was completely withdrawn from Moscow society. She made no calls and received none. She would not even meet the families of her sons- and daughters-in-law. Her domestic world was limited to servants and the seven of her eleven children who were still living at home.

There was one exception—Nicholas Rubinstein, Director of the Moscow Conservatory, a fine musician even though overshadowed somewhat by his famous brother Anton.

Rubinstein was always a welcome visitor, but on this December afternoon of 1876 he had not come merely for a social chat. In his portfolio was the piano arrangement of "The Tempest," a fantasia by a thirty-seven-year-old teacher at the Conserva-

11

tory, Peter Ilyich Tchaikovsky. If Mme von Meck would care to hear it . . .

Rubinstein sat down at the big Steinway grand piano. He was not disconcerted to find himself alone with the gilt chairs and brocaded sofas from Paris. He was well aware that it was Mme von Meck's habit to listen to music from another room, sitting in darkness.

Rubinstein played well. In later years, Tchaikovsky was to maintain that no one understood his music as did Nicholas Grigorievich. Then Rubinstein got round to the purpose of his visit.

This Peter Ilyich Tchaikovsky; a gifted composer, but as poor as he was gifted; too proud to truckle for recognition and too shy to push his own works. . . . As a consequence he was in desperate financial straits. His conservatory salary, eked out by private teaching, was inadequate. He lived in Rubinstein's house and the Director sometimes aided him with the gift of a dress coat or a dozen shirts. Still the wolf remained at Tchaikovsky's door.

Would Nadejda Filaretovna, who had aided so many musicians, help Tchaikovsky? Not with an outright gift; the composer was too proud and touchy for that. Perhaps she might commission something.

Tchaikovsky's situation was not unknown to Nadejda Filaretovna. Although a recluse, she had excellent sources of information. Her household retinue always included a musician, whose duties were to play duets with her and to give music lessons to her children. Later, this post was to be occupied by "my little Parisian," Claude Debussy.

In 1876 the incumbent was Josef Kotek, who as a student at the Conservatory had formed an intimate friendship with Tchaikovsky. He had told Mme von Meck a great deal about Peter Tchaikovsky. He had also told Tchaikovsky a great deal about Nadejda Filaretovna.

Tchaikovsky, who liked whatever was original and unconventional, took the liveliest interest in what Kotek told him of the recluse of the Boulevard Rojdestvensky. No doubt he could hardly believe his own good fortune when he received his first commission from Mme von Meck.

Details of this first commission have been lost. Modeste Tchaikovsky, the composer's brother and biographer, says only that he was to make piano-and-violin arrangements of "several of his own works," for which he received "a high fee."

Tchaikovsky's work evidently gave satisfaction, for on December 30, 1876, Mme von Meck sent him this letter:

HONORED SIR—Permit me to express my sincere thanks for your speedy execution of my commission. I feel it superfluous to tell you of the enthusiasm I feel for your music, since you are doubtless accustomed to receiving homage very different from any which could be offered you by so insignificant a person, musically speaking, as myself. It might therefore seem absurd to you; and my admiration is something so precious that I do not care to have it laughed at. I shall accordingly say only one thing, which I beg you to accept as the literal truth—that your music makes life easier and pleasanter to live.

Tchaikovsky replied next day:

HONORED MADAME—I thank you most cordially for the kind and flattering things you have written to me. For my part, I can assure you that, among all his trials and failures, it is a great comfort to a musician to know that there are a few people—of whom you are one—who are true and passionate music-lovers.

Soon thereafter Tchaikovsky received another commission, which he lost no time in executing. The acknowledgement was dated February 27, 1877:

DEAR SIR, PETER ILYICH—I do not know how to thank you for your kind indulgence of my impatience. If it were not for my deep sympathy toward you, I should fear that you would spoil me, but I appreciate your kindness too greatly for this to happen.

I should like to tell you a great deal about my fancies and feelings toward you, but I fear to take up your leisure, of which you have so little to spare. Let me say only that my feeling for you is spiritual and very dear to me. So, if you will, Peter Ilyich, call me erratic, or even mad, but do not laugh at me—all this would be laughable if it were not so sincere and real.

Again Tchaikovsky replied by return mail:

DEAR MADAME, NADEJDA FILARETOVNA—Accept my hearty thanks for the too-generous fee with which you have repaid such a trifling task. I am sorry you hesitated to tell me all your thoughts. I assure you I should have been most interested and pleased, since I for my part feel deeply sympathetic toward you. These are not empty words. Perhaps I know you better than you suppose. . . .

Nadejda Filaretovna needed no further encouragement. The correspondence which followed was one of the most extraordinary in history. For fourteen years, by mail and private messenger, letters went back and forth almost daily between Peter Ilyich and Nadejda Filaretovna. The major part of their correspondence has been preserved and in published form fills three large volumes.

Tchaikovsky's letters afford an insight into his working methods and states of mind such as few other composers have left behind them. The correspondence is a treasure-trove for program annotators.

Musical matters, however, were almost incidental in what was essentially an ardent yet platonic love affair by correspondence. Formal salutations quickly gave way to terms of endearment—"Dear Nadejda Filaretovna"—"My dear and invaluable friend"—"Kind and beloved Nadejda Filaretovna." Abélard and Héloïse hardly poured out their souls more unreservedly than did these two shy, misanthropic people in their letters to one another.

But they never met.

2

MODESTE TCHAIKOVSKY, in his biography of his famous older brother, remarked that certain flaws in the composer's character were the result of having been spoiled as a child.

Tchaikovsky began life in comfortable circumstances. He was born in a two-story mansion in Votkinsk, a town on the border between the provinces of Vyatka and Perm, on May 10, 1840. Votkinsk was what would be called in America a "company town"; its principal industry consisted of its iron mines and metallurgical works, chief inspector of which was Lieutenant Colonel Ilya Petrovich Tchaikovsky. As chief inspector Colonel Tchaikovsky was in effect ruler of the town and surrounding countryside. He had well-defined legal and police powers, enforceable by his troop of one hundred Cossacks.

Colonel Tchaikovsky married the first of his three wives in 1827. By her he had a daughter, Zinaida, whose name is hardly mentioned in the Tchaikovsky family's correspondence. His second wife, Alexandra Andreyevna Assier, had a thorough knowledge of French and German, played the piano a little and sang nicely. "A satisfactory education," wrote her son Modeste, "for a girl who had neither means nor position."

The couple had five sons—Nikolay, Peter, Hyppolite and the twins Modeste and Anatole—and a daughter, Alexandra. To teach the older children, a French governess named Fanny Dürbach had made the three-week journey from St. Petersburg. Four-year-old Peter Ilyich begged to join the lessons too, and astonished Fanny by his precocious intelligence.

Even more astonishing, in a family not remarkable for musicality (brother Hyppolite's ear was so undiscerning that in after years when Peter Ilyich's music was played he would have to be informed of the fact), was Peter's extraordinary musical gift. He was improvising as soon as he was able to sit at the piano, and composed his first song at four. When he could not get to the piano, he drummed out tunes with his fingers on a windowpane. Once, completely absorbed in the music he was hearing mentally, he broke the glass and cut his hand severely.

Fanny Dürbach tried to discourage the boy's preoccupation with music. She felt his hyper-sensitivity to musical sounds to be morbid and unhealthy. Once, after a party which the children had been allowed to stay up to attend, she found Peter sitting up in bed, weeping. "The music, the music!" he cried. "Save me from it. It's in there"—tapping his head—"and it won't let me rest."

The nervous, morose temperament which was to characterize the adult Tchaikovsky was already evident in the boy. He cried easily, and moped aimlessly about the house when separated from his music. One of his mother's letters noted that "Petya is unrecognizable, he's lazy, does nothing. I don't know what I shall do with him. He often makes me cry."

Another trait which showed itself early was his adoration of Russia and all things Russian. Fanny recalled that once during a geography lesson he covered the map of Russia with kisses and spat on the rest of Europe. When Fanny remonstrated, he said: "There is no need to scold me—I covered France with my hand."

Nothing annoyed the adult Tchaikovsky more than the suggestion that his family origins were Polish. (Tchaikovsky, while not an unknown name in Russia, in Poland is as common as Smith.) But whatever his antecedents, Tchaikovsky himself was Russian as a samovar. He loved Russian architecture, Russian art, the pomp and splendor of the Russian Orthodox service, the Russian folk tunes which occur so frequently in his music.

Yet, ironically, many of his serenest moments were to be spent outside Russia. St. Petersburg depressed him, Moscow meant responsibilities which galled and irked him. In his letters, time after time, there is an almost audible sigh of relief when he has put the Russian frontier behind him. He would never be happier than when in some distant city, Florence for example, looking out over the Tuscan landscape and occasionally shedding tears of homesickness for the faraway frozen steppes.

Tchaikovsky's earliest musical influences included an amateur named Mashovsky who played Chopin with dash; a piano teacher named Marya Markovna Palchikova, whom he soon outstripped at sight-read ing; and a now-obsolete household instrument, the "orchestrion," which could play *"Vedrai carino"* from *Don Giovanni* and works of Rossini, Donizetti and Bellini. It was through this machine that Tchaikovsky acquired his lifelong passion for Mozart. In later years he said that it was because of Mozart that he had devoted his life to music.

In 1848 there was an upheaval in the Tchaikovsky household. Ilya Tchaikovsky resigned his position at Votkinsk and was retired from government service with the rank of major general. To a colleague he revealed in strict confidence the reason for the move: A splendid new appointment was awaiting him in Moscow.

In October, 1848, the Tchaikovsky family made the long journey to Moscow. There a blow awaited them; the trusted colleague had made use of Ilya Tchaikovsky's information to secure the appointment for himself.

In Moscow there was an epidemic of cholera, that fierce Asiatic scourge which even today is a killer with an eighty per cent mortality rate. In November the Tchaikovsky caravan moved on to St. Petersburg. Here Ilya Petrovich obtained a position as manager of factories in Alapayevsk, on the Siberian border. He took his family there the following May.

In 1850 his parents decided to enter ten-year-old Peter Ilyich in the School of Jurisprudence in St. Petersburg. He arrived there with his mother in September, 1850.

The parting with his mother Peter Ilyich regarded as the most dreadful experience of his life. He had to be separated from her by main force. When her carriage started, he broke away from those holding him and tried to cling to the turning wheels. Years afterward he shuddered when he described the scene.

But youth is resilient, and Peter Ilyich was soon working at his studies with commendable zeal. His marks were excellent except in religion, Latin and mathematics. He was popular with his fellow students. What most of them remembered about him was his intense personal charm, his slovenly appearance and his almost feminine sensitivity. His black moods were endured in the privacy of his room, or communicated in letters to Mademoiselle Fanny, now governess in another family.

Peter Ilyich was re-united with his family in May, 1852. Ilya Petrovich had had enough of Alapayevsk. His savings and his government pension would enable him to live modestly at St. Petersburg. Although Peter Ilyich was still a boarding student at the School of Jurisprudence, he had the pleasure of spending his Sunday *exeat* at home.

In June, 1854, a month after Peter's fourteenth birthday, both his parents were stricken with cholera. Ilya Tchaikovsky's life was despaired of, but he recovered and lived to be eighty-five. Alexandra Andreyevna rallied briefly, but a relapse forced the kill-or-cure therapy of a hot bath. It killed.

The impact of his mother's death on Tchaikovsky may be judged from the fact that more than two years elapsed before he could bring himself to write to Mademoiselle Fanny about it.

In his adolescent misery, Tchaikovsky turned to music as if to an anodyne. He composed a waltz, which has not survived; took singing lessons from the choral conductor, Gavril Akimovich Lomakin; studied piano under a prominent teacher named Rudolf Vasilyevich Kündinger, who assured Ilya Petrovich his son had no spark of genius, though possessing unusual powers of improvisation and some harmonic sense; attended plays and concerts; and absorbed the backstage lore of the opera house from an odd transplanted Neapolitan named Piccioli, who dyed his hair black and denied the name of music to everything but the operas of Rossini, Donizetti, Bellini and the promising newcomer, Verdi.

Young Peter Ilyich was to much a Mozart-idolater to exclude Mozart from this divine circle, and too thoroughly Russian to exclude Glinka; but he listened and did not contradict Piccioli, whom he found more stimulating than his cut-and-dried studies at the School of Jurisprudence.

In 1857 the Tchaikovsky family circle received another shock. Ilya Petrovich lost his money. Details which have survived are scanty. Modeste said it was "through over-confidence in humanity." Peter Ilyich, writing to Mme von Meck long afterward, was a little more explicit. His father had been "retired and lived on the income from the small capital that he had accumulated after many years of service. In 1857 he put that sum in the hands of an adventuress who promised him mountains of gold, and lost all of it that very year, irrevocably."

Whatever the circumstances of the transaction, Ilya Petrovich was cleaned out, and at sixty-three had to look for a job again. Fortunately he was soon appointed Director of the St. Petersburg Technological Institute.

On May 13, 1859, Peter Ilyich, just turned nineteen, was graduated thirteenth in his class at the School of Jurisprudence, and received a diploma entitling him to the rank of government clerk. At his own request, he was attached to the Ministry of Justice.

Although Tchaikovsky's heart was not in his work, he made rapid enough progress to be promoted in seven months to the rank of junior assistant, and, three months later, to senior assistant to the chief clerk.

Once Tchaikovsky was on his way to deliver an important document when he met a friend. All his life Tchaikovsky had the curious habit of tearing papers, usually theatre programs or ticket stubs, to bits and chewing the pieces as he talked. On this occasion the talk was a long one, and at its conclusion Tchaikovsky had to go back to his office for a new copy of the document. When his chief asked what had happened to the original, Tchaikovsky was obliged to confess that he had eaten it.

3

THE TCHAIKOVSKY FAMILY circle was growing smaller. Nikolay and Hyppolite had left home, Hyppolite to enter the Navy—he would eventually become an admiral. On November 18, 1860, Alexandra married Lyov Vasilyevich Davidov and went to live with him at Kamenka, the Davidov estate near Kiev. The twins were in school and Peter Ilyich was plugging away in the Ministry of Justice, oppressed by the conviction that he was frittering away his time to no purpose.

It was kindly Ilya Petrovich, concerned over his son's all-too-apparent unhappiness, who suggested in March, 1861, that it was not too late for him to take up a musical career. Gloomily Peter Ilyich shook his head. He knew, far better than his father, what such a career entailed. He had had a great deal of exposure to music, but it had been desultory, unsystematic. Worst of all, there was no real evidence of talent, aside from his unswerving love of music. He had no voice; his beautiful boy-soprano had changed to a colorless goat-bleat baritone. He had started too late to be a concert pianist. As for composing, that was the most absurd of all. He was nearly twenty-one and had had no systematic training in harmony and counterpoint, the ABC's of composition. At twenty-one, Mozart had already put a quarter of his voluminous output behind him. . . .

Ilya Petrovich did not press the point, but did not let it drop either. The thought presently occurred to Peter Ilyich that he might study composition privately. To do this it would not be necessary to burn his bridges behind him by leaving the Ministry of Justice.

His first teacher was Nikolay Ivanovich Zaremba, who was the instructor for classes sponsored by the Imperial Russian Musical Society. Zaremba had been trained in the thoroughgoing school of Germany and expected his students to measure up to the same technical standard. Tchaikovsky's studies at first were perfunctory, until Zaremba took him aside and bluntly told him to get to work. He had a fine talent; it would be a pity to waste it.

This was just the prodding Tchaikovsky needed. Later, Modeste would write: "I recollect having made two discoveries at this time which filled me with astonishment. The first was that the two ideas 'Brother Peter' and 'work' were not necessarily opposed; the second, that besides pleasant and interesting music, there existed another kind, exceedingly unpleasant and wearisome, which appeared nevertheless to be the more important of the two. I still remember with what persistency Peter Ilyich would sit at the piano for hours together playing the most abominable and incomprehensible preludes and fugues. My astonishment knew no bounds when he informed me he was writing exercises. It passed my understanding that so charming a pastime as music should have anything in common with the mathematical problems we loathed."

Peter Ilyich was also studying scores, widening his knowledge of the classic and contemporary repertory. All his time which could be spared from the Ministry of Justice was devoted to music. He cut himself off from the gay life usual among young men in government service. Puzzled by his monomania, his friends, one by one, dropped him.

In 1862 a big musical project was under way. The Imperial Russian Musical Society was to open a conservatory. The moving spirits behind the plan were the German-born Grand Duchess Elena Pavlovna, aunt of Tsar Alexander II, and the pianist Anton Rubinstein.

A friendship had existed between the two since 1849. In that year Elena Pavlovna, a forty-two-year-old widow, had installed the twenty-two-year-old pianist as music-master in her villa on Kammenoi-Ostrow (Stone Island) in the Neva, for which Rubinstein was to name one of his most popular piano works. Gossip buzzed when the two traveled about Europe together.

Now, in 1862, the Grand Duchess persuaded her Imperial nephew to give his blessings to the conservatory project, and to subsidize it as well. Rubinstein was the Director. The faculty included Henri Wieniawski, violin virtuoso and composer of some of the most fluent works, from a performer's point of view, ever written for that instrument; Theodor Leschetizky, who was to make the name "Leschetizky pupil" an international *cachet* in pianistic circles; and the 'cellist and composer Karl U. Davidov.

On September 20, 1862, the St. Petersburg Conservatory opened its classes in what had been a luxurious private home. Among the first to matriculate was Peter Ilyich Tchaikovsky.

Two days after the conservatory opened, Peter Ilyich wrote prophetically to his sister Alexandra: "Sooner or later I shall abandon my present job for music."

The break came in the spring of 1863. Alexandra thought her brother insane to throw up the security of his government post, and said so in a letter to Ilya Petrovich. Peter's reply explained the reasons for his decision. His musical flair—she could not deny it—was his only talent. That being so, he ought not to leave this God-sent gift uncultivated and undeveloped. At first his studies had not interfered with his job, and he had been able to remain at the Ministry of Justice. "Now, however, my studies grow more severe and take more time, so that I find myself compelled to give up one or the other. . . . After long consideration, I have resolved to sacrifice the salary and resign my post. But it does not follow that I intend to get into debt, or ask for money from Father, whose circumstances are not very flourishing just now. . . . I hope to obtain a small post in the conservatory next year (as assistant professor); secondly, I have a few private lessons in view; and thirdly—what is most important of all—I have entirely renounced all amusements and luxuries, so that my expenditure has very much decreased.

"Now you will want to know what will become of me when I have finished my course. One thing I know for certain. I shall be a good musician and shall be able to earn my daily bread. The professors are satisfied with me and say that with the necessary zeal I shall do well."

He cherished a dream, he added; "to come to you for a whole year after my studies are finished to compose a great work in your quiet surroundings. After that—out into the world."

Although Tchaikovsky never got to Kamenka for a year, he was to turn out creditable quantities of work in briefer visits to the Davidov estate.

In the atumn of 1863, after visiting a friend named Apukhtin, Tchaikovsky returned to the conservatory. His father had moved to a smaller apartment and could give him nothing but bare board and lodging. He earned a few rubles of pocket-money from private piano students whom Anton Rubinstein found for him.

Despite his pinched circumstances, Tchaikovsky was happy. His hitherto aimless life had taken on purpose and direction. Modeste asserted that "the sacrifice of all the pleasures of life did not in the least embitter or disturb him. On the contrary, he made light of his poverty, and at no time of his life was he so cheerful and serene as now. In a small room, which only held a bed and a writing-table, he started bravely on his new, laborious existence, and there he spent many a night in arduous work."

At the conservatory Tchaikovsky was excused from the normally-required course in piano. It was realized that his hands were not those of a solo performer, and that his real forte was composition. Under Zaremba he underwent a stiff course in counterpoint, and under Anton Rubinstein an equally rigorous training in free composition.

The extraordinary personality of Rubinstein appears to have fascinated all his students at the conservatory. Tchaikovsky's attitude to the Director was outright hero worship. This fact increased his zeal in carrying out Rubinstein's assignments. The harder the tasks set before him, the more energetic Tchaikovsky became. Sometimes he worked through the night on a score which he wished to show to his insatiable teacher next day. Even Rubinstein was astonished by his pupil's industry. "Once in the composition class I told him to work out contrapuntal variations on a given theme," Rubinstein recalled, "and mentioned that in this sort of work not only quality but quantity was important. I thought that he might write about twelve variations. Not at all. At the next class he gave me over two hundred."

In one matter, however, Tchaikovsky maintained independence of judgment. Rubinstein prided himself on being pedantically old-fashioned in orchestration. The largest combination permissible to a student was composed of strings, paired woodwinds, trumpets and three trombones—the Mozart-Haydn orchestra, with trombones added.

Tchaikovsky, however, as every bar of his orchestral music shows, was fascinated by the piquant sounds which the Boehm system of keys for woodwinds, valve-horns, and other products of nineteenth-century ingenuity were placing at the disposal of the composer.

In the summer of 1864 Tchaikovsky was assigned

a holiday task, that of writing an overture for Ostrovsky's drama, *The Storm.* (The overture was published posthumously as his Opus 76). He scored the piece for a "heretical" orchestra which included tuba, English horn, harp and tremolo for violins *divisi.* When the score was finished he mailed it to his fellow student Herman Augustovich Laroche with the request that he place it before the Director.

"Never in the course of my life," said Laroche, "have I had to listen to such a homily on my own sins (it was Sunday morning too!). With unconscious humor, Rubinstein asked: 'How dared you bring me such a specimen of your own composition,' and proceeded to pour such vials of wrath upon my head that apparently he had nothing left for the real culprit. When Peter Ilyich himself appeared a few days later, the Director received him amiably, and only made a few remarks upon the overture."

Laroche was present when Tchaikovsky made his debut as a conductor. The advanced composition students were expected to take turns in leading the school orchestra, and Tchaikovsky was first in the class.

Although in later years Tchaikovsky became quite a passable conductor and was in demand as an interpreter of his own works, when he first stood on the podium before the school orchestra he was numb with shock. He told Laroche his nervousness produced the sensation that his head was about to fall off his shoulders. The sensation was so vivid that he was obliged to hold his left hand under his chin while he conducted with his right.

Several years later Laroche heard Tchaikovsky

conduct at a charity concert in Moscow. "I still see him before me," said Laroche, "the baton in his right hand, while his left firmly supported his fair beard!"

Tchaikovsky's final, oral examination at the conservatory was scheduled for January 10, 1866. When the day arrived, Tchaikovsky was so terrified at the prospect of being quizzed in public that he failed to appear. This enraged Anton Rubinstein, who threatened to hold up the awarding of his diploma. But eventually the Director simmered down. Tchaikovsky received his diploma and a silver medal.

He had served a hard apprenticeship at the conservatory, but he left it well equipped for his life's work. Whatever the grounds on which his music has been criticized, they have not included lack of skill in manipulating the materials of music.

4

HARD TIMES were now in store for Tchaikovsky. He was depressed by his perpetual shortage of money, so different from the circumstances of his early life. Anton Rubinstein had persuaded him to translate Gevaert's *Treatise on Instrumentation* (1863) into Russian, and he found the task to be tedious and uncongenial. At this low moment a friend proposed, and Tchaikovsky seriously considered, trying for the secure salary of a government inspector of meat.

One encouraging event was the first performance of his orchestral work, "Dances of the Serving-maids." It was played at an outdoor concert in Petropavlosky Park, under the renowned Johann Strauss, Jr., and was warmly received.

Even more encouraging was an offer to teach at the new conservatory founded in Moscow, in the fall of 1866, by Anton Rubinstein's younger brother, Nicholas. Although his faculty was not so brilliant as that assembled by Anton, Nicholas had counted on having as his Professor of Harmony the composer A. N. Serov. But, after accepting the post, Serov had been performed in St. Petersburg and Moscow. Finding himself cheered in St. Petersburg and hissed in Moscow, Serov had decided to stay in St. Petersburg.

Nicholas appealed to Anton, who recommended Tchaikovsky as a substitute.

In Moscow, Tchaikovsky came into contact with two men who were to play an important part in his life both as man and artist. One of them was Peter Ivanovich Jurgenson, a native of Revel on the Baltic coast who, after a poverty-stricken childhood, at nineteen had gone to work in a music warehouse in St. Petersburg, at twenty-three had become general manager of the Moscow publishing firm of Schildbach and two years later had gone into business for himself.

Jurgenson was Tchaikovsky's first and virtually his only publisher. Of the 200,000 engraved plates in his fireproof safe, Modeste would record later, 70,000 were works of Tchaikovsky.

The other close association was with Nicholas Rubinstein. If Tchaikovsky's feeling for Anton was hero worship, he could regard the younger Rubinstein, only five years his senior, as a friend, for whose musical judgment he had high respect. Although the friendship was to be severely strained at times, it would end only with Rubinstein's death.

Since Tchaikovsky's salary at the conservatory obviously would not suffice for living quarters, Rubinstein took the new Professor of Harmony into his home. There Tchaikovsky immediately set to work orchestrating the Overture in C Minor which he had composed the previous summer.

Very early Tchaikovsky manifested a trait which was to be unchanged throughout his career. He could always work, anywhere, at any time. Yielding and pliant in so many other respects, in this he was inflexible. With regard to his work, he once wrote to Mme von Meck: "my will is iron." In Moscow, or visiting the Davidovs at Kamenka, he toiled regularly, at fixed hours, and was much annoyed if anything disrupted his working routine.

Tchaikovsky had no patience with dilettantism, a fact which was to color his relationship with the "Mighty Five" in St. Petersburg. Although he adored Glinka, whose *Russlan and Ludmilla* and *A Life for the Tsar* marked the beginning of the nationalistic school of Russian music, he attributed the unevenness of Glinka's music to the fact that he was an aristocrat dabbler who worked only when inspiration moved him. Tchaikovsky believed in meeting inspiration halfway.

Now, newly arrived in Moscow, he was doing just that. "I am very busy," he wrote to Modeste. "I sit at home nearly all day, and Rubinstein, who leads rather an excitable life, cannot sufficiently marvel at my industry."

"Excitable" was the word for Rubinstein. He never stopped. After a day's hard work at the conservatory he was ready to spend the evening pursuing the light ladies of Moscow, or in gambling for high stakes at the English Club until dawn. "He had a dreamy expression," said his friend N. D. Kashkin, "a languor of speech and an air of aristocratic weariness, which was contradicted by the indefatigable energy of his temperament. Probably this languor proceeded from the fact that he scarcely ever slept."

Rubinstein had worked his way through Moscow University by giving piano lessons. He soon became Moscow's foremost teacher, at one time earning seven thousand rubles a year from piano pupils. (Tchaikovsky's beginning salary at the conservatory was fifty rubles a month.) On his marriage to a well-connected Moscow lady he had given up playing in public; his wife's family felt it to be undignified. After two years the marriage had ended in divorce. Free again, Rubinstein had busied himself with teaching, performing, conducting concerts and promoting all sorts of musical schemes, the most ambitious of which was the conservatory. He had the organizer's talent and was, said Kashkin, "acquainted will all circles of Moscow society, commercial, official, artistic, scientific and aristocratic."

Something like the attraction of opposite polarities must have accounted for the friendship between the convivial, energetic director of the conservatory and the shy, introspective Professor of Harmony. In one respect, Rubinstein discovered in Tchaikovsky social talent equal to his own. Tchaikovsky, noted Rimsky-Korsakoff glumly in his memoirs, could drink the "Mighty Five" under the table, singly or en masse.

Tchaikovsky delivered his first lecture at the conservatory clammy with stage fright. Somehow he survived the ordeal, and a month later could write to Alexandra: "My classes are very successful, to my great astonishment; my nervousness is vanishing completely, and I am gradually assuming the airs of a professor."

This was pure bluff, and no doubt intended to reassure Tchaikovsky himself as well as his sister. Tchaikovsky hated teaching. In the first place, it took up time which could be more valuably spent in composing. Secondly, he considered himself unqualified to teach. In this he was mistaken. His students adored him. His greatest asset, according to those who attended his classes, was his phenomenal musical memory. He was never at a loss for musical examples, often drawn from obscure and long-forgotten works, to illustrate any point which came up in class discussion.

In the spring of his first year at the Moscow Conservatory Tchaikovsky began sketching his Symphony No. 1 in G Minor ("Winter Daydreams"). No other work, said Modeste, cost him such pains as this one. Tchaikovsky had never before grappled with sonata form on a large scale. Adept though he was in what could be called short-range musicality, the inventing of melodies and setting them forth in appropriate harmonic and orchestral garb, in creating the over-all pattern his hand was unsure. Try as he might, he could not make the pieces fit his grand design.

Writing, revising, slashing out what he had done and starting afresh, Tchaikovsky labored over his First Symphony. It was the busiest time of his conservatory year. There were final examinations to be given, papers to be corrected, grades to be awarded. Tchaikovsky had mountains of paper work to dispose of before turning to his own composing. Sometimes he worked straight through the night, à la Rubinstein.

He began to suffer from hallucinations. Sleep, when he could snatch it, was a nightmare. In his waking hours he was oppressed by a strange, indefinable sense of dread.

At the end of June, 1867, his overtaxed constitution gave way. He suffered a complete nervous breakdown. The physician who attended him declared that he had narrowly escaped insanity, and that his condition was still extremely serious. Complete rest was prescribed; and no more composing until at least the end of the summer.

The experience gave Tchaikovsky a salutary scare. Never again would he attempt to work through the night.

5

IN THE AUTUMN, refreshed by his summer holiday, Tchaikovsky returned to Moscow. One of his first acts was to submit his "Winter Daydreams" Symphony to his old composition teachers in St. Petersburg, Anton Rubinstein and Zaremba.

To his chagrin, both men found fault with the symphony, criticizing in particular those passages of which the composer was most proud. Against his better judgment, Tchaikovsky revised the symphony to suit their ideas. The two middle movements were performed at a St. Petersburg concert, and fell flat.

Later in the season Tchaikovsky restored the work to its original form, in which it was performed at a Moscow concert with considerable success.

This episode led to a cooling of Tchaikovsky's affection for St. Petersburg and his former musical associates there. It also brought him for the first time into contact with the Five.

The Moscow program on which Tchaikovsky appeared also had included Rimsky-Korsakoff's "Serbian Fantasy." A review which appeared in *The Entr'acte* praised Tchaikovsky, but dismissed Rimsky-Korsakoff as "lifeless and colorless."

During rehearsals Tchaikovsky had become acquainted with the "Serbian Fantasy," and he disagreed vehemently. He wrote a stinging rebuttal which, published in *The Entr'acte*, created a sensation, both in Moscow and St. Petersburg. When Tchaikovsky went up to visit his father at Easter, the Five welcomed him with open arms.

There was never a genuinely intimate musical friendship between Tchaikovsky and the Five. Their artistic philosophies diverged too widely. During the early years under Balakirev's leadership, the Five, had gone over completely to the view that an artist needed only his inspiration as a guide. If one had inspiration, one had no need of dry counterpoint exercises. Tchaikovsky, having had an old-fashioned, formal music education, and now being a conservatory professor, was in their eyes a pedant.

Tchaikovsky for his part regarded the Five as dilettantes, all of whom composed music as a sideline. His letters bristle with unflattering references to the "Invincible Band." Balakirev, it was true, had shown flashes of dazzling originality; and his suggestion for a "clash of swords" to open Tchaikovsky's "Romeo and Juliet" had so pleased Tchaikovsky that he had dedicated the finished work to Balakirev. Later on, however, a series of personal crises had distracted Balakirev from composition.

Borodin was "unable to get his music down on paper without someone else's help." He was, moreover, preoccupied by his duties as a professor of chemistry. Cui's music had a certain grace and elegance, but his output was small. Moreover, he had deeply wounded Tchaikovsky by his hostile reviews. Years later the touchy Tchaikovsky was able to recite, word for word, the bad notice Cui had written on his G Minor Symphony.

For Mussorgsky, Tchaikovsky felt only contempt. He was a musical ruffian who did not know anything, did not want to learn anything and looked down on persons who did. For Tchaikovsky, an amateurishly-written passage was "a smudge à la Mussorgsky."

The member of the "Invincible Band" for whom Tchaikovsky had most respect was Rimsky-Korsakoff. And the feeling was reciprocated. When Rimsky-Korsakoff, feeling himself held back by inadequate technique, began the systematic study of composition, it was Tchaikovsky's manual of harmony which he used as a textbook. When, in an incredibly industrious summer, Rimsky-Korsakoff turned out sixty-four fugues, it was Tchaikovsky to whom he submitted ten of them for criticism.

Whatever the divergence in their musical views, the social relations between Tchaikovsky and the Five were pleasant. Also, Tchaikovsky set himself the task of promoting their music in Moscow by amiable log-rolling whenever possible, a friendly act which the Five reciprocated for Tchaikovsky in St. Petersburg.

Tchaikovsky's early years at the Moscow Conservatory were relatively uneventful. He taught harmony, he traveled, he widened his circle of friends, and above all, incessantly, he wrote music.

The First Symphony was followed by a second, in C Minor, and a third, Symphony in D ("Polish").

None of these represented the mature, fully-evolved Tchaikovsky, and they are played so infrequently that an old joke runs:

"Q. How many symphonies did Tchaikovsky write?

A. Three; the Fourth, Fifth and Sixth."

Three operas belong to this period, *The Voyevode, The Oprichnik* and *Vakoula, the Smith*. None was a success, although the overture to *The Voyevode* is heard occasionally and *Vakoula,* in a later and revised version, has been performed in New York as *Les Caprices d'Oxane.*

Another opera, *Undine,* was finished but never performed. Eventually Tchaikovsky destroyed the score, after borrowing its best parts for use in other works.

Tchaikovsky's first group of songs, published as Opus 6, included the famous "None but the Lonely Heart." Soon afterward he wrote the First String Quartet in D, probably the best-known work in the entire chamber music repertory. Its celebrated and thrice-familiar Andante Cantabile, which according to Tchaikovsky made Tolstoy cry when the composer played it for him, was based on a folk song which Tchaikovsky heard a gardener singing outside his window while he was visiting the Davidovs at Kamenka.

Another big work of this period was the Piano Concerto in B-flat Minor. Tchaikovsky's account of the work's inception was as follows:

"In December, 1874, I wrote a piano concerto. As I am not a pianist, I needed a virtuoso's opinion as to what was technically impractical, difficult, unplayable, and so on. I needed a serious but friendly critic, but only for the pianistic aspect of my composition. Rubinstein is not only the first pianist of Moscow, but is truly a perfect pianist; knowing he would be deeply offended if he thought I had ignored him, I asked him to listen to the concerto and give me an opinion on the piano part, although some inner voice protested against my selecting him as judge."

Rubinstein assented, suggesting that since they were both invited to the same Christmas Eve party they meet beforehand in a classroom at the conservatory.

"I played the first movement. Not a word, not a remark. If you only knew how disappointing, how unbearable it is when a man offers his friend a dish of his work, and the other eats and remains silent! Well, say something—scold, in a friendly way, but for God's sake, one sympathetic word, even if uncomplimentary. . . . The point was that I did not want a verdict on artistic merits, but advice as to piano technique. Rubinstein's eloquent silence had great significance. As much as to say—'My friend, can I speak of details when the thing as a whole disgusts me?'

"I armed myself with patience, and played it through to the end. Again silence. I stood up and said, 'Well?'

"Then from the lips of N. G. R. poured a torrent of words, first quiet, then more and more the tone of Jupiter, master of the thunderbolts. It appeared that my concerto is worthless, impossible to play, the themes have been used before, are clumsy and awkward beyond possibility of correction; as a composition it is poor. I stole this from here and that from there, there are only two or three pages that can be salvaged, and the rest must be thrown away or changed completely!

" 'For example, that—well, what is that?' (And he plays the place indicated, exaggerating it). 'And that? Is it possible?' And so on. An outsider, dropping into the room, would have thought me a madman, without talent, ignorant, a worthless writer who had come to annoy a famous musician with his rubbish. . . .

"I was not only astonished but offended by the performance. I am no longer a boy, trying his strength in composition—I no longer need lessons, especially lessons expressed so sharply and in such a hostile manner. I need, and will always need, friendly criticism, but this was nothing like friendly criticism. It was a decisive, blanket condemnation, expressed in such a manner as to touch me in a sensitive spot.

"I walked out of the room without a word and went upstairs. I was speechless with excitement and fury. Rubinstein appeared soon after, and seeing my disturbed state of mind, called me to another room. There he repeated that my concerto was impossible, and, having pointed out many places needing radical change, told me that if I would alter the concerto according to his wishes by a certain date, he would do me the honor of performing it at his concert. 'I shall not change a single note,' I replied, 'and will print it exactly as it stands.' And so I did."

But the sequel was that fifteen years later Tchaikovsky reworked the piano part completely, and the concerto, no longer a "duel for piano and orchestra," was played with great success by all the leading pianists of Europe—including Nicholas Grigorievich Rubinstein.

Tchaikovsky's account of the concerto was written later to Mme von Meck, with whom, of course, he was not acquainted at the time of its composition. But she was soon to enter his life and to affect its course profoundly.

6

Nadejda Filaretovna Frolowsky von Meck was born in 1831, thus being nine years older than Tchaikovsky. Her father was a landowner and a district judge. Her mother had been a Potemkin, a collateral descendant of the famous Gregory who had been the lover of Catherine the Great.

Nadejda Filaretovna's mother has been described as "a woman of great force"; her father, as "a quiet man who played the violin." The traits of both recurred in their remarkable daughter.

Music was part of Nadejda Filaretovna's childhood. She accompanied her father's violin-playing, and played four-hand piano duets with her sister.

At seventeen Nadejda Filaretovna married Karl George Otto von Meck, a descendant of the Teutonic Knights of Riga—Germans who had pushed north and conquered the Baltic provinces centuries before. Karl George had an impressive lineage and little else. His father had run through his patrimony; the estate of Zunzel, in the family for centuries, had had to be sold; very early, Karl George had been left a penniless orphan. When he entered the School of Engineering in St. Petersburg he had been obliged to travel the hundred miles from Riga on foot.

On his graduation he was assigned to a post near

Smolensk, where he met and married Nadejda Filaretovna. The marriage appears to have been a happy one, but after Nadejda Filaretovna had borne five children in five different towns, she issued an ultimatum. She had had enough of this nomadic life which led nowhere. The bureaucracy was a dead-end street. The imperious Potemkin heritage asserted itself. Something would have to be done.

Nadejda Filaretovna herself told the story in a letter to Tchaikovsky:

I have not always been rich. The greater part of my life I was poor, very poor indeed. My husband was an engineer in the Government service, with a salary of 15,000 rubles a year— which was all we had to live on, with five children and my husband's family on our hands. Not a brilliant prospect, as you see! I was wet-nurse, governess and dressmaker to my children and valet to my husband; the housekeeping was entirely in my hands; naturally there was plenty of work, but I did not mind that. It was another matter which made life unbearable.

Do you know, Peter Ilyich, what it is to be in the Government service? Do you know how, in that case, a man must forget that he is a reasonable being, possessed of will power and honorable instincts, and must become a puppet, an automaton? It was this I found so intolerable that finally I implored my husband to send in his resignation. To his objection that if he did so we should starve, I replied that we could work and that we should not die of hunger. When

at last he yielded to my desires, we were reduced to living upon twenty kopecks a day for
everything. It was hard, but I never regretted
for a moment what had been done.

And at last Karl George Otto von Meck turned
the narrow corner, going on to become a sort of
Russian Commodore Vanderbilt. His genius was for
building railroads. His still-surviving map of Russia,
with probable routes of future railroads drawn in,
shows a vision amounting almost to prophecy.

But Karl George had a poor head for business.
He was unable to estimate a contract. On his first
engineering venture he "bid too low on the job," as
the saying goes, and in consequence lost every cent
of his savings and his wife's dowry to boot. Thereafter Nadejda Filaretovna took over management
of financial affairs.

Under this arrangement the von Mecks prospered.
Karl George built a railroad from Moscow to Ria-
zan; his sons Nicholas and Vladimir were later to
extend it as far eastward as the Ural Mountains.

Karl George died in his fifties, leaving Nadejda
Filaretovna two railroads, several million rubles, the
mansion on the Boulevard Rojdestvensky, an estate
called Brailov in the Ukraine, and eleven children,
ranging in age from four to twenty-four.

Newly widowed, Mme von Meck sat down to con-
sider her situation and to chart the future course of
her life. Her financial circumstances were such that
she was not obliged to do anything which she found
tedious or unpleasant. This meant among other

things that she would no longer have to go out in society.

Oddly, and somewhat paradoxically, this energetic, ambitious and determined woman, who had blasted her husband out of the rut of officialdom and helped to establish his fortune, was almost morbidly shy. (It was this shared trait which had interested her in Tchaikovsky.) Using her widowhood as a pretext, she immured herself within the four walls of her home. This confinement was by no means arduous; "home" could mean the big house in Moscow, her country estate of Brailov, a villa on the French Riviera or almost any other place which her fancy dictated. With a few exceptions like Nicholas Rubinstein, she saw and spoke to no one but her servants, her children, and, as the years passed, her sons- and daughters-in-law and grandchildren. All these, however, were numerous enough to keep her well occupied. An early morning at Nadejda Filaretovna's must have been remarkably like the levée scene in *Der Rosenkavalier*.

Such was the lady who responded with almost schoolgirlish eagerness to Tchaikovsky's suggestion that she reply more fully in her next letter.

Their correspondence continued, as it had begun, on a note of lover-like intimacy. "There was a time," wrote Nadejda Filaretovna in her third letter, "when I earnestly desired your personal acquaintance; but now I feel the more you fascinate me, the more I shrink from knowing you. . . . At present I prefer to think of you from a distance, to hear you speak and to be at one with you in your music."

"You are quite right, Nadejda Filaretovna," the composer replied, "in thinking that I am able to understand your inward mind and temperament. I venture to believe that you have not made a mistake in considering me a kindred spirit."

They debated as to which of them was the more shy; Nadejda Filaretovna maintained it was she. "I am positive I shall win," she wrote, "first, because I am older than you, and second, because I have severed relations with the world so completely that I never speak to people in hotels and shops; everywhere I go, I pretend not to understand the language. Once in Russia—and in our own native tongue—somebody asked me right out if I was Madame von Meck, and I said, No, there must be some mistake."

On May 12, 1877, five months after the beginning of their correspondence, Nadejda Filaretovna proposed that Tchaikovsky compose an original work for violin and pianoforte. The fee which she mentioned was described this time by Modeste as "extravagant."

Tchaikovsky can hardly have failed to be tempted by the fee. At the moment he was in unusually severe financial straits. On the other hand, as he was later to tell Nadejda Filaretovna, he had come to dislike the sound of piano and strings. Also, the musical program she supplied—the piece was to express the grief of having "lost what you loved and held dear"—made clear that he would be writing a sort of requiem for the late Karl George Otto von Meck.

In addition, he had a big work in hand which he was loath to interrupt. And, finally, he had a shrewd suspicion that Kotek, taking advantage of his status as violinist in residence, had had a hand in arranging the commission.

He said as much to Nadejda Filaretovna: "In spite of obstinate denials on the part of a friend [Kotek, says Modeste Tchaikovsky] who is well know to both of us, I have good reason to suppose that your letter, which I received early this morning, is due to a well-intentioned ruse on his part. Even your earlier commissions awoke in me a suspicion that you had more than one reason for suggesting them: on the one hand, you really wished to possess arrangements of some of my works; on the other—knowing my material difficulties—you desired to help me through them. The very high fees you sent me for my easy tasks forced me to this conclusion. This time I am convinced that the second reason is almost wholly answerable for your latest communication."

While touched by her kindness and delicacy, he added, he could not accept the commission. He also mentioned that he was working hard at a symphony begun during the winter, and asked permission to dedicate it to her. This was the first reference in their correspondence to the Fourth Symphony, which would soon be known as "our symphony."

Nadejda Filaretovna was not at all put out by Tchaikovsky's refusal to compose "The Reproach" (this was the title she had selected). She immediately sent Tchaikovsky three thousand rubles to pay the most pressing of his debts.

"I am looking after you for my own sake," she wrote. "My most precious beliefs and sympathies are in your hands; your very existence gives me so much enjoyment, for life is the better for your letters and your music. . . ."

Not long thereafter, Mme von Meck made the proposal that they use the intimate form of speech with one another. In English, "thou," "thy" and "thee" are so obsolete that one uses them, if at all, solely when addressing his Maker. In languages preserving the second person singular, it is the form used for childern, for servants or a lover.

Tchaikovsky boggled at this suggestion. Their relationship, he replied, was so perfect that he wished to keep it exactly as it was.

Nadejda Filaretovna was forty-six, not old as time is ordinarily reckoned. Throughout the correspondence there are coy touches which hint that, had Tchaikovsky wished, he could have battered down Mme von Meck's defenses like papier-mâché.

But Tchaikovsky had no intention of doing so, for a reason which was soon to put Nadejda Filaretovna's devotion to the severest test imaginable.

7

Tchaikovsky looked forward to Nadejda Filaretovna's letters, and was unhappy when they were slow to arrive. Once, he wrote to his brother Anatole; "Mme von Meck had not written me for a long time, and with my usual misgivings I imagined that she had ceased to love me, that she had found out about *The*, and wanted to break off all connection."

In Holy Writ, homosexuality is "The abomination of desolation." In Tchaikovsky's confidential letters to Modeste and Anatole, it is simply *"The."*

Tchaikovsky was a homosexual. So was Modeste, and so was Tchaikovsky's nephew, Vladimir (Bob) Davidov, the confidant of the composer's last years.

Anatole, Modeste's twin, was not, although he of course knew the significance of *"The."* So did Alexandra; Peter Ilyich wrote to Modeste: "I know that she guesses everything, and forgives everything."

Tchaikovsky in this respect was unique among major composers. Others, to a man, left no doubt of their virility.

In 1868 an Italian opera company headed by an impresario named Merelli (presumably the same Merelli who commissioned Verdi's earliest works) had visited Moscow. "The company," says Laroche, "consisted of fifth-rate singers, who had neither voices nor talent; the one exception was a woman of thirty, not good-looking, but with a passionate and expressive face, who had just reached the climax of her art, and soon afterward began to go off, both in voice and appearance. The timbre of her voice was penetrated by such indescribable beauty, warmth and passion that everyone who heard it was fascinated and carried away."

This was the soprano Desirée Artôt. Tchaikovsky heard her sing Desdemona in Rossini's *Otello* and was carried away like everyone else. He called on her; was cordially received; and soon fell into the habit of going to her house every day. On January 7, 1869, he had written to his father that he and Mlle Artôt were to be married.

There were a number of obstacles, he admitted. Her mother opposed the marriage, supposing he would expect her to live permanently in Russia. His friends, especially Nicholas Rubinstein, raised many objections. She was famous, he was not; she had money, he had none; he would be dragged ignominiously all over Europe as a prima donna's husband; and so on.

Ilya Petrovich sent a wise and affectionate reply: "As a father I rejoice; Desirée is surely worthy because my son Peter loves her, and my son Peter is a man of taste and talent who would naturally select a wife with like qualities. . . . Friends and sympathizers fear that your career will be sacrificed to this marriage; I disagree. You who for your talent's sake gave up a career in the Government

Service surely will not, at the first momentary disappointment, cease being an artist."

When the opera company left Moscow, Tchaikovsky considered himself to be engaged. That Artôt did not was shown by the fact that a month later, while appearing in Warsaw, she had married a Spanish baritone named Mariano Padilla y Ramos.

Twenty years later, Tchaikovsky wrote Modeste from Berlin that he had found himself next to Artôt at dinner. "She was in evening dress and fat as a bubble. We were friends instantly, as though the past had never been. I was inexpressibly glad to see her and found her as fascinating as ever."

Despite the outcome of this romance with Artôt, in which he appears to have been more fascinated by Artôt the artist than physically attracted to Artôt the woman, Tchaikovsky continued during the intervening years to toy with the idea of marriage. Among other things, it would put an end to gossip. Tchaikovsky may well have been aware that there was talk regarding himself and Joseph Kotek, which possibly had got back to the Davidovs.

"In a word," he wrote Modeste in the fall of 1876, "I should like to marry, or by some known liaison with a woman, shut the mouths of all despicable gossips, for whose opinions I do not care a bit, but who can hurt people close to me."

He looked forward, he confessed, to marriage with aversion, as to a painful but necessary operation. "What comfort—I could almost say joy—there is in returning to my pleasant quarters and sitting down with a book in my hands! At this moment I detest, probably no less than you do, that beautiful, undiscovered being who will make me alter my manner of living."

Nevertheless his mind was made up, and he was determined that "I shall make a serious effort to marry, legally, anybody. I am aware that my inclinations are the greatest and most unconquerable obstacle to happiness. I must fight my nature with all my strength. . . . I shall do everything possible to marry this year, and if I am not brave enough for that, at any rate I shall conquer my old habits once and for all."

Modeste must have urged caution before taking so drastic a step as marriage. Tchaikovsky replied: "The realization of my plans is not so near as you think. I am so deeply mired in my tastes and habits that to discard them all at once, as one would discard an old glove, is impossible. Besides, I am far from being made of iron. Since my recent letters to you, I have already succumbed to my natural inclinations three times."

Soon after, the correspondence with Nadejda Filaretovna began. Once she asked a rather searching question, which Tchaikovsky parried with exquisite finesse:

"You ask if I have known non-platonic love. Yes and no. If the question were put a little differently, have I felt the happiness of fulfilled love, the answer would be no, no, no!! I think the answer to your question lies in my music." And he was back on safe ground. His music, he said, would tell better than words how he felt about love.

In the spring of 1877 Tchaikovsky was busy with

his Fourth Symphony and still preoccupied with the idea of getting married. In May he wrote to a friend, the architect and musical amateur, I. A. Klimenko: "Since last we met I am very much changed—especially mentally. Not a kopek's worth of fun or gayety is left in me. Life is terribly empty, tedious and tawdry. My mind turns toward matrimony or indeed any other steady bond."

On June 7, Nadejda Filaretovna wrote to Tchaikovsky from Brailov. He had asked whether he might dedicate his Fourth Symphony to her. She had never given such permission before. Could he, without naming her by name, dedicate it simply to his "Friend"? That is, if he considered her a friend; he had never, she pointed out, said so in so many words. . . .

She had to wait more than a month for an answer. Toward the middle of July an envelope arrived in the handwriting of her composer-correspondent, and this bombshell tumbled out:

"For God's sake, dear Nadejda Filaretovna, forgive me for not writing before. Briefly, here is the story of what has lately happened to me.

"In the latter part of May, to my own great surprise, I became engaged to be married. . . ."

Nadejda Filaretovna's reaction on learning that her dear friend, while pouring out the innermost secrets of his heart without reservation, had withheld this particular bit of information, does not have to be imagined. It has been preserved in her own words:

"Do you know what when you married it was terribly hard for me, as though something had broken in my heart? The thought that you were near that woman was bitter and unbearable. And do you know what a wicked person I am? I rejoiced when you were unhappy with her! I reproached myself for that feeling. I don't think I betrayed myself in any way, and yet I could not destroy my feelings. I hated that woman because she did not make you happy, but I would have hated her a hundred times more if you had been happy with her. I thought she had robbed me of what should be mine only, because I love you more than anyone and value you above everything in the world."

But it was more than two years later when she made this confession. Her immediate action was to write a gracious note:

"With all my heart I congratulate you, my dear friend, on the new step, a step that is always a gamble. . . ."

Of this fine example of the stiff upper lip, Catherine Drinker Bowen has written: "Remember, this was no casual woman, casually bred. This was a gentlewoman; behind her, generations of women who had learned restraint, generations of ladies who did not cry when they were hurt."

It was well for the music still unwritten that this was so; otherwise his marriage might have been the end of Tchaikovsky.

8

Antonina Ivanovna Miliukova was twenty-eight, but looked not more than twenty-three. Herbert Weinstock apparently has erred in describing her as a student at the conservatory; according to Tchaikovsky she was educated at the Elisabeth Institute, a girls' secondary school in Moscow, and "educated not above the average." When they became acquainted, she was working, and living apart from her family. Tchaikovsky was somewhat astonished to find that she knew almost nothing of the music he had written.

She had seen or met Tchaikovsky somewhere and had become infatuated with him. Early in 1877 she wrote him a letter telling him so. "It was written so sincerely and warmly," Tchaikovsky told Nadejda Filaretovna, "that I was led to do what in such cases I had always carefully avoided—to answer. Although my answer did not give any hope that the feeling could be mutual, the correspondence started. I will not tell you in detail about it, but the result was that I consented to go to see her. Why did I? I now feel as if Fate had drawn me to that girl. When I met her I again explained to her that I felt no more thàn sympathy and gratitude for her love. And when I left I began to think over all the giddiness of my behavior. If I did not care for her, if I did not want to encourage her, why then did I go to see her, and how will it all end?"

Tchaikovsky, struggling in the toils, tried to break off the relationship, whereupon Antonina Ivanovna threatened to kill herself. "Let me look at you and kiss you," she wrote, "so I may carry that kiss into the other world."

At this Tchaikovsky was panic-stricken: "I had a difficult alternative—to save my freedom at the price of the girl's ruin (ruin is not an empty word; she really loves me to distraction)—or to marry. I could not do otherwise than choose the latter. One thing that helped me to a decision was the fact that my eighty-two-year-old father and all my relatives live in the hope of having me marry. So one fine evening, I went to my future wife, told her frankly that I did not love her, but that I would be a devoted and grateful friend, described my character in detail, my irritability, my variable temperament, unsociability, and finally my circumstances. Then I asked her if she would be my wife. The answer, of course, was 'Yes.'"

Weinstock has an ingenious theory that Tchaikovsky, at this time deep in the imaginary world of *Eugene Onegin*, saw Antonina Ivanovna through a romantic haze as a real-life Tatiana, artlessly pouring out her heart to the man she loved, and could not bring himself to play the callous role of Onegin by rebuffing her.

But he must have cautioned her not to expect too much in the way of romantic ardor. He had told her he felt no more than "sympathy and gratitude" for her love, and had promised only to be "a devoted and grateful friend." Perhaps he could not bring himself to tell her, fully and frankly, about *"The."* Perhaps Antonina Ivanovna was too naïve to understand. Or perhaps she believed this obstacle would be overcome by her irresistible charms. Antonina Ivanovna was under the delusion that every man she met fell head over heels in love with her, a delusion which was to have pathetic consequences later on.

Tchaikovsky delayed writing to Nadejda Filaretovna about his impending marriage until three days before the ceremony. He delayed almost as long in writing to his family (Ilya Petrovich said the news "made me so happy I crossed myself and jumped for joy"). Consequently they were unable to attend the wedding. When Tchaikovsky and Antonina Ivanovna were married at the Church of St. George in Moscow, on July 18, 1877, the only witnesses were Anatole and the violinist Joseph Kotek.

A quaint photograph of the newlyweds exists. It shows Antonina Ivanovna as a well-developed young woman with a pretty face and figure; and Tchaikovsky, looking more like a scared rabbit than a composer whose name was known as far away as Boston, staring into space as if recoiling from the prospect before him.

The marriage of a homosexual to an incipient nymphomaniac is a situation rich in low-comedy possibilities, but to Tchaikovsky, as one of the participants, it was anything but funny. "As the train started," he wrote to Anatole of his wedding trip, "I was on the point of screaming, choked up with sobs. In spite of that, I had to talk entertainingly with my wife as far as Klin in order to buy the right to remain, alone with myself, in my own chair in the dark. . . . The only mitigation was that she did not understand or recognize my poorly concealed agony."

It is more than likely that Tchaikovsky remained on the point of screaming until August 7, when he fled from Moscow, alone. An appeal to Nadejda Filaretovna had been a cry *de profundis*. He had to get away, to rest, to think. His wedding had taken all his money. There was no one else to whom he could turn. Would Nadejda Filaretovna lend him a thousand rubles?

Nadejda Filaretovna, at Brailov, sent the money by return post. "Go to the Caucasus," she wrote, "and go quickly. . . . Think of me sometimes, enjoy nature, be quiet and happy. I hope your next letter will explain more fully. . . ."

It did. He and his bride, Tchaikovsky wrote, had gone to St. Petersburg to visit Ilya Petrovich; then to call on his wife's mother, who lived near Moscow. He had taken an instant dislike to his in-laws, whom he found rather commonplace; "they have narrow and freakish opinions and are constantly quarreling. My wife (this may be unfair) became more abhorrent to me each hour."

His nerves were so on edge that he could not work. He had fortified himself by drinking a good deal of wine, "which made me dizzy," and by "cheering talks with Kotek." But the situation could not go on indefinitely. He had seriously considered suicide, but the thought of his father, Alexandra and the twins had made him desist. And, moreover, he loved life, loved his work, loved the prospect of success. He had not yet written a tenth of all he wanted to write, and which he might yet accomplish with the help of the "hundred-times-priceless friend who is saving me. Nadejda Filaretovna, if God gives me the strength to get through the terrible present, I shall prove to you that this friend has not helped me in vain."

Tchaikovsky arrived at Kamenka on August 12. On seeing the pitiable state of his nerves, his sister urged him to give up his trip to the Caucasus. At first he was too distraught to work. Ten days in familiar surroundings, among familiar faces (Anatole and Modeste were visiting Kamenka also) soothed him to the point of beginning the orchestration of the Fourth Symphony.

He spent six serene weeks at Kamenka. Once more he was able to work. "Our symphony progresses," he wrote to Nadejda Filaretovna. "I am much better. I feel sure I shall now triumph over my difficult and critical situation."

"I hope as you do," Nadejda Filaretovna wrote, "that after some rest, some time passed among people with whom you have so much in common"— a suave thrust at the Miliukovs with whom he had so little in common—"you will regain your strength, and find things not so bad as you thought."

But the return to Moscow could not be postponed any longer. On September 11 he wrote to Nadejda Filaretovna: "The weather grows more and more autumnal. The fields are bare, and it is time I took my departure. My wife writes that our rooms are now ready."

Antonina Ivanovna met him at the railway station. "I know you are wondering how I feel now," he wrote to Anatole next day. "Tolia! Don't ask me—I am frightened—that is all I shall say. I was too happy in Kamenka, maybe that is why the contrast seems so sharp. . . ."

On September 24, Tchaikovsky made his appearance at the conservatory. "He had an exaggeratedly carefree and bold manner, but that was obviously put on," his fellow professor, N. D. Kashkin, recalled. "Noting his nervous state, we were all very careful, asked no questions, and waited for him to introduce us to his wife." Tchaikovsky did so, at a supper given by his publisher, Jurgenson. Kashkin said that Antonina Ivanovna "created a generally favorable impression, both by her appearance and her modest manner."

Tchaikovsky's piano had been installed in the living room of their apartment, but he could do no work. He was later to describe this period as one of "unbearable torment." After a week of it, one evening he waded waist-deep into the icy waters of the Moscow River, too irresolute to drown himself, but hoping to catch pneumonia and die.

He told Antonina Ivanovna he had joined a fishing expedition and fallen overboard. Only Kashkin heard the true story.

Tchaikovsky was again on the verge of insanity, and now knew it. On the morning of October 6, says Kashkin, he appeared at the conservatory looking "strangely agitated. He said he had been summoned to St. Petersburg by the conductor, Napravnik, and took hasty leave of his colleagues." Actually he had asked Anatole to telegraph him in Napravnik's name.

Anatole said that his brother was scarcely recognizable when he met him on the platform of the Nicholas Station in St. Petersburg. His face had entirely altered in the course of a month. Anatole rushed him to a room in the near-by Dagmar Hotel, where after a violent attack of nerves he sank into a coma and remained unconscious forty-eight hours. The doctors hastily summoned by Anatole ordered a "complete change of life and scene" as Tchaikovsky's sole hope of recovery.

Eight days later Peter Ilyich was recovered enough to board a train for Switzerland with Anatole. At Clarens, on Lake Geneva, there was a reassuring letter from Nicholas Rubinstein: "Try to calm yourself; take care of your health and fear nothing. You are far too highly valued as a musician to be compromised by secondary considerations."

On the material side, he was not to worry. An advance against his conservatory salary was being sent. This was good news; Tchaikovsky had money enough to last only five or six weeks. Also, said Rubinstein, "I have seen Mme von Meck. We talked a great deal about you. I think she will send you another commission, or money direct."

Nadejda Filaretovna did even better. She informed Peter Ilyich that she was settling on him an annual income of six thousand rubles to enable him to devote himself entirely to composition.

Tchaikovsky's reaction to this news can be imagined. He was no longer dependent on the conservatory; he need never go back to Moscow—or to Antonina Ivanovna.

"I do not suppose," he replied to his benefactress, "that I shall ever have an opportunity of proving that I am ready to make any sacrifice for you in return; I think you will never be compelled by circumstances to demand any supreme service from my friendship; therefore I can only please and serve you by means of my music. Nadejda Filaretovna, every note which comes from my pen in future is dedicated to you!"

Now, with money in hand, it was possible to plan for the future. Modeste had taken a position as tutor to a deaf-and-dumb boy named Conradi. They would join Peter Ilyich and spend the winter with him in Italy. (Later, Kotek turned up too. He had been dismissed by Mme von Meck for gossiping too freely about her correspondence with Tchaikovsky. Peter Ilyich had interceded for Kotek, but in vain.)

Anatole would then go back to Moscow to put his brother's affairs in order, and see what could be done about Antonina Ivanovna.

At present she was staying with the Davidovs. Alexandra had gathered up the weeping, abandoned bride and taken her to Kamenka. In the beginning Alexandra's sympathy appears to have been with Antonina Ivanovna. Well knowing what it was that unsuited her brother for marriage, and having tried to dissuade him from it, she could hardly regard the girl except as victim of a rather cruel hoax.

Closer acquaintance changed her mind. Antonina Ivanovna was a weeper; she wept without apparent cause for days on end. She was a compulsive nail-biter; blood from nails bitten to the quick spattered her letters, spattered the books from which she tutored the Davidov children. One hesitated to occupy a chair or sofa vacated by Antonina Ivanovna; there was always blood where she had been sitting.

She was extremely talkative, but her conversation was solely about the number of men who had been in love with her, mostly generals, nephews of famous bankers, well-known actors or members of the Imperial family (at Kamenka, she told Anatole, a colonel had fallen in love with her)—or about the detestable behavior of her relatives, particularly her mother.

Her attention-span was as limited as a child's. She was incapable of sticking to anything for an hour. When her hostess queried her about future plans, she cheerfully admitted she had none. She liked Kamenka and intended to stay. Besides, she had nowhere else to go. At the moment she was not on speaking terms with her mother, her relatives or any of her friends.

When Anatole was about to return to Moscow from Italy, he received a note from Lyov Davidov. It was a pressing invitation to stop off at Kamenka—and, by the way, to take Antonina Ivanovna back to Moscow with him.

Anatole did. He also sounded out Antonina Ivanovna about a divorce. It was obvious that Peter Ilyich, if he were to retain his sanity, could not live with her again. Antonina Ivanovna agreed, then changed her mind. At that time adultery was the sole legal ground for divorce in Russia. A divorce could be obtained, as in New York State today, by collusion, but Antonina Ivanovna may be pardoned for wanting no part of such a messy business. She went into hiding; Jurgenson tracked her down. In a conversation which, the publisher said, went round and round like a squirrel in a cage, she first agreed to divorce, then said if Peter Ilyich were charged with adultery she would go into court to attest his innocence.

Meanwhile she bombarded her husband with vituperative letters and with requests for money. Tchaikovsky paid.

Some time later, the tireless Jurgenson made a discovery. Antonina Ivanovna had taken a lover named Bolkov, by whom she had had a child, and was living with Bolkov in Moscow.

This news brought inexpressible relief to Tchaikovsky. Now, if Antonina Ivanovna tried blackmail, he could counter-attack.

From time to time there were reports of other children, of uncertain paternity. Nevertheless, to the end of his life Tchaikovsky continued to pay for most or all of her support. Legally she was still his wife.

Antonina Ivanovna's final years were calm; they were spent in an asylum.

9

IN SAN REMO, waiting for Modeste and his deaf-mute pupil to join him, Tchaikovsky pushed ahead with *Eugene Onegin*. Although his ill-advised marriage had driven him to the brink of insanity, in the midst of the turmoil he had somehow completed the Fourth Symphony and the first act of *Onegin*, and both works were on their way to Moscow.

Modeste and "Kolia" Conradi arrived; so did Alexis Safronov, who was to be Tchaikovsky's personal servant for the remainder of his days. The four traveled to Florence, where they visited churches and museums, and where Tchaikovsky picked February violets to mail to Nadejda Filaretovna in snow-bound Moscow. And, incessantly, Tchaikovsky worked.

On February 13 the remaining portion of *Eugene Onegin* was in the mail. As soon as the opera was finished, Tchaikovsky commenced his violin concerto. Kotek had arrived, and was able to give an opinion as to whether this or that passage lay well for the instrument. On April 11, Tchaikovsky wrote Nadejda Filaretovna that he had finished the violin concerto that morning.

His health was improving, he told her, but he still needed quiet if he was to return to the conservatory in September. He would visit the Davidovs at Kamenka.

There, "Uncle Petya" received his usual hearty welcome. Antonina Ivanovna's visit had made clear that the fault was not exclusively on Peter Ilyich's side.

Tchaikovsky also accepted an invitation from Nadejda Filaretovna to visit Brailov. She herself would not be there.

To Tchaikovsky the 12,000-acre estate, with fields, forests, gardens, a river for boating, saddle-horses and carriages for driving, was like a fairyland. He told his absent hostess so in daily letters, and left for her three violin pieces, "Souvenir d'un lieu cher."

In September Tchaikovsky was back at his familiar grind of teaching twenty-six hours a week. After his freedom of the past few months, he found the burden intolerable. Also, he had received a tempting offer from St. Petersburg: four hours a week, at double his Moscow salary; and instead of explaining to a class of forty beginners that a triad consists of a third and a fifth, he would work with only a few talented students from the advanced class. But it was impossible to accept the offer: Nicholas Rubinstein's feelings would be hurt.

Early in October, Rubinstein himself returned from Paris, where he had been Russia's musical representative at the 1878 Exposition. There was a great testimonial dinner to honor the pianist, whose playing had created a sensation in Paris.

Rubinstein arose in response to a toast. Not he, but Tchaikovsky had been the hero of the Paris Exposition. Not his playing, but Tchaikovsky's music, had conquered. The Piano Concerto had taken the Parisians by storm. . . .

The stunned composer was obliged to make a speech in reply. "I came home absolutely desperate," he wrote Nadejda Filaretovna. After this public tribute, it would be the most blatant ingratitude to withdraw his name from the conservatory. But his teaching days were over, and he knew it. He no longer needed his conservatory salary, thanks to Nadejda Filaretovna's generosity. He appealed to his "precious, beloved friend." What should he do?

Nadejda Filaretovna's reply was prompt and unhesitating. Leave the conservatory by all means; go abroad. "I too shall spend the winter abroad. If you could come somewhere near me, dear friend, how happy it would make me!"

Tchaikovsky assented eagerly; and there followed perhaps the most idyllic part of the curious relationship between the curious pair.

When Tchaikovsky arrived in Florence, he found Nadejda Filaretovna had engaged for him a lavish five-room suite at the Villa Bonciani, half a mile from her own villa. A fine grand piano was in the drawing room, flowers were everywhere, and on the desk was a warm note of welcome, including the information that she took her daily walk, past the Villa Bonciani and a little beyond, every morning precisely at eleven o'clock. (Without this information, she doubtless reasoned, Peter Ilyich would be afraid to venture out.)

As a matter of fact, Tchaikovsky wrote to Anatole: "On the journey here I was troubled with the thought that Nadejda Filaretovna would be living so close to me; that we might meet. I even had a momentary suspicion that she might invite me." And, if she asked him to call, he would of course have to do so. "But a letter from her, which I found on my writing-table yesterday, set my mind at rest. She will be leaving in three weeks, and during that time probably we shall not see each other once."

He was wrong. One afternoon, out walking, he came face to face with two ladies in an open carriage. He recognized them instantly from photographs which Nadejda Filaretovna had sent him. The one in white was her married daughter, Lydia Karlovna. And the one in black was Nadejda Filaretovna herself.

Tchaikovsky bowed, doubtless with his heart in his mouth. Would the carriage stop? It did not; Nadejda Filaretovna was nearsighted and had not realized who it was.

A few nights, later, however, she saw him at the opera; at least she had thought it was he, sitting near the trumpets and trombones. It was, Tchaikovsky wrote back; and he had seen her with her daughter Milochka; he had watched them through his opera glasses. "What can she have been telling you? She never stopped talking for a second, and with such animation! Is there anything more captivating than the face of a charming child?"

Back and forth the letters went, by Alexis or the violinist Pahulsky, to whom Tchaikovsky was giving counterpoint lessons. Pahulsky had taken Kotek's place as Nadejda Filaretovna's private musician, and was later to marry her daughter Julia.

By correspondence they discussed Pahulsky's progress and argued about the merits of Lalo and Mozart. On December 17 Tchaikovsky reported that "with fear and trembling" he had begun a new opera, based on Schiller's *Maid of Orleans.*

They were seeing each other frequently; sometimes at the theatre—or, Tchaikovsky, watching from his window, might see Nadejda Filaretovna walk past with her children, the German governess and Milochka's black poodle. Or the Von Mecks, during their morning walk, might hear Tchaikovsky working at the piano.

Tchaikovsky may have felt himself to be living dangerously; but Nadejda Filaretovna was enchanted. "How I love you!" she wrote. "Rising in the morning, my first thought is of you, and all day I am conscious that you are near; your presence seems to inhabit all the air about me! This is where I want to be; your nearness is a never-ending delight. Dear one, you won't leave Florence before I do?"

There is no telling what all this might have led to; but it was time to go. Nadejda Filaretovna began to marshal her children, governesses, maids, butler's helpers, cooks, lackeys and coachmen. (In Vienna, twenty rooms had been reserved for her at the Hotel Metropole.)

After her departure, Tchaikovsky moped about Florence like a lost soul. "How recently I was embarrassed by her close proximity," he wrote to Anatole, "and now I miss her!"

Nadejda Filaretovna had been so charmed by their Florentine stay that the following spring she urged Tchaikovsky to visit her at Brailov. There

was an abandoned farmhouse called Simaki which
was two miles from the main house, and which
could be put in order for his own exclusive use. His
privacy would, as always, be respected. In nineteen
square miles of farmland and forest there would
surely be room enough so that they would not get
in each other's way; and to make doubly certain
she would inform him ahead of time where she
planned to go each day.

It would have been impossible to refuse so gracious an invitation unless there were extremely
urgent reasons for being elsewhere. Besides, Tchaikovsky had fallen in love with Brailov on his earlier
visit. And it had been a long, hard winter. *Eugene
Onegin* had been brought out in Moscow with only
moderate success. His "Tempest" Overture, based
on Shakespeare's play, had been hissed in Paris.
And Tchaikovsky, who had been present, had sufficient artistic honesty to know the Parisians had
been right. "The Tempest" was a good idea which
had not quite come off. He said as much in a
letter to Edouard Colonne, the conductor, adding
that the work had been well prepared and conductor and orchestra were in no wise to blame for
the fiasco. The letter, when published, won much
praise for the "modesty and sincerity" of the composer.

Altogether, a difficult, unsettling winter, during
which he had nevertheless made progress with *The
Maid of Orleans*. It would be good to get to the
country, rest, and work undisturbed.

"I am enchanted," he wrote to Nadejda Filaretovna from Simaki. "I could not imagine more beau-

tiful surroundings." He described them to Modeste:
"A very, very old house, a shady garden with ancient
oaks and lime trees; it is very secluded, but therein
lies its charm. At the end of the garden flows a
stream. From the veranda there is a fine view over
the village and the forests. The absolute quiet and
comfort of the place exactly suit my taste and re-
quirements. I have at my disposal an old man-
servant called Leon, a cook whom I never see, and
a coachman with a phaeton and four horses. I could
gladly dispense with the latter, since it requires
driving occasionally, whereas in reality I prefer to
walk."

But even this earthly paradise was not without a
flaw. "The presence of Nadejda Filaretovna troubles
me somewhat, although this is really folly. I know
my seclusion will not be disturbed. I am so accustomed to regard her as a kind of remote and invisible geni that her mortal presence in my neigh-
borhood is rather disconcerting."

Nevertheless, he intended to keep Nadejda Filaretovna at arm's length, and her family as well. The
counterpoint lessons with Pahulsky had resumed,
and once the violinist proposed to bring little Milochka to his next lesson. Tchaikovsky squelched
this idea. He wished everything about his relationship to the von Mecks to remain exactly as it was,
he wrote to Nadejda Filaretovna. If he met Milochka in person, "the charm would be dispelled."
And what if Milochka should ask why he did not
call on her mother? He would be compelled to
tell a lie, which he would find hard. "Forgive me,
my own dear wonderful friend, for my frankness."

Pahulsky was no longer welcomed at Simaki.

Mrs. Bowen believes it was Milochka who schemed to bring about the accidental meeting with Tchaikovsky, by delaying dinner past the usual hour. Mrs. Bowen's description of the two carriages meeting face to face is contradicted by Tchaikovsky's letter to Anatole:

"Yesterday something very painful happened. About four o'clock in the afternoon I was walking in the woods, feeling sure I should not meet Nadejda Filaretovna, because it was her dinner hour. It chanced, however, that I went out a little earlier, and she was dining somewhat later, so we ran against each other quite by chance. It was an awkward predicament. Although we were face to face only for a moment, I felt horribly confused. However, I raised my hat politely. She was in one carriage with Milochka, and the whole family followed in two others. I wandered into the forest in search of mushrooms, and when I returned to the little table where tea was prepared for me, I found my letters and newspapers awaiting me. It appears she had sent a man on horseback after me, so that I might get my mail at teatime."

Nadejda Filaretovna was charmed by this accidental meeting; but Tchaikovsky's reaction was so obviously stark panic that she felt it necessary to send a reassuring note: "I don't seek any close personal relationship with you, but I love to be near you passively, tacitly—to be under the same roof with you, as in the theatre in Florence, and to meet you on the road. To me these occasions are extraordinary good fortune."

On September 8, 1879, four days before his departure for St. Petersburg, Tchaikovsky wrote Nadejda Filaretovna that he was completing *The Maid of Orleans.* He had been working at the score, along with other things, since the previous December, in Florence. "It is remarkable that I began and finished this opera as the guest of my dear friend."

10

DURING THE eighteen-eighties Tchaikovsky found himself growing rich and famous. The Violin Concerto had joined the First Piano Concerto as an indispensable part of the repertory of every virtuoso. The Fourth Symphony was making its triumphant way about the concert halls of Europe and America. *The Maid of Orleans* had been a failure, and *Eugene Onegin* had made little headway outside Russia; but the latter was popular in Moscow and St. Petersburg.

Tchaikovsky began to receive offers from publishers in Paris, Berlin and Leipzig. Although some of them were tempting, he refused, and told Nadejda Filaretovna why: Jurgenson had published him when the name of Tchaikovsky meant nothing. "Up to now I have not earned him a cent, because while a few of my things sell well, others lie forever on the shelves of his warehouse. He bases all his calculations on the hope that some day my reputation will cross the frontier and my works will move freely in the European market. So now that my name is becoming known in Europe, would it not be unfair to confine Jurgenson's profit on my works to Russia?"

Tchaikovsky's letters were postmarked from Moscow, St. Petersburg, Paris, Rome, Berlin. He was traveling constantly, supervising opera rehearsals, attending first performances of his works, and, eventually, conducting them himself.

He had screwed up his courage sufficiently to conduct the revised version of *Vakoula the Smith*. He conducted the first orchestra rehearsal, he told Modeste, in such style that all were astonished, "unless it was mere flattery."

Conducting, he wrote Nadejda Filaretovna, "gives me great anxiety and exhausts my whole nervous system. But I must say it also affords me great satisfaction. First of all, I am very glad to have conquered my innate, morbid shyness; secondly, it is a good thing for a composer to conduct his own work, instead of having constantly to interrupt the conductor to draw his attention to this or that mistake; thirdly, all my colleagues have shown me such genuine sympathy that I am quite touched by it, and very pleased."

Tchaikovsky was always at his best as a conductor when this bond of sympathy existed between himself and the musicians. If their attention wandered, if they appeared to be bored, he was incapable of recalling them to duty in the traditional stentorian conductor's manner. His inclination was to cut short the rehearsal, in order to free the musicians from their distasteful task as soon as possible.

For diversion Tchaikovsky sought the blue skies and warm sunlight of Italy. On a visit to Rome he stayed next door to the barracks of a troop of cuirassiers. A fanfare blown by the bugler fascinated him; he jotted it down and later used it as the opening of his "Capriccio Italien."

In Nice, Tchaikovsky learned that Nicholas Rubinstein was ill and traveling to Paris to get away from the Moscow winter. While the doctors could not agree on a diagnosis, they agreed Rubinstein should be kept in bed, an obvious impossibility.

"He is a perfect contrast to you and me," Tchaikovsky wrote Nadejda Filaretovna. "In proportion as we love seclusion, he loves to walk about the world and roar. He simply cannot live without excitement and rushing about; it is life to him. He dislikes reading, to walk bores him and he even has no pleasure in making music for himself—others must be there to listen. What can rest and tranquillity give such a man? Nothing but torture."

When Tchaikovsky got to Paris, he learned that Rubinstein was dead. In its coffin the familiar face was almost unrecognizable. "My God, my God," Tchaikovsky wrote Nadejda Filaretovna, "how terrible are such moments in our lives!"

But there was no time to grieve. Duty summoned him to Moscow. Among other things there was the question of who was to succeed Rubinstein at the conservatory. Tchaikovsky himself was urged to take the post, but refused. His choice was his former pupil, S. I. Taneyev, who eventually became the new Director.

There were social engagements, which exhausted Tchaikovsky but which he had not the courage to decline. He was paying the price of fame. The Grand Duke Constantine stopped his carriage to talk to Tchaikovsky, and to invite him for a trip around the world on a Russian battleship.

Occasionally there were droll experiences, like the Caspian Sea voyage during which Tchaikovsky agreed to be accompanist at a shipboard entertainment.

(He had taken elaborate pains to conceal his identity.) An amateur vocalist explained to him in detail how one of his own songs ought to be performed. When Tchaikovsky ventured to differ, the young lady assured him that hers was the correct interpretation; her teacher had it from Tchaikovsky himself.

He apologized to Nadejda Filaretovna for writing so infrequently, and explained the reason: "I have to start on my concert tour abroad. I conduct first in Leipzig, and afterwards in Dresden, Hamburg, Copenhagen, Berlin and Prague. In March I give my own concert in Paris, and from there I go to London, as I have received an invitation from the Philharmonic Society."

From Paris he wrote to Modeste that his travels exhausted him. "Even the knowledge that I start for Russia tomorrow brings no satisfaction, *because I have no home anywhere.* I cannot go on living the life of a wandering star. Where will my *home* be?"

Not at Brailov; the estate had been sold by Nadejda Filaretovna during a period of financial hardship. She continued his annuity, however, explaining that it was as nothing compared to the millions which had been lost.

Kamenka was quieter; the children were growing up; Alexandria had been attacked by the long illness which would end with her death; Tatiana, the spoiled and willful favorite niece, a drug addict and pregnant by her music teacher before she was twenty, had collapsed and died at a masked ball in St. Petersburg. Kotek was fighting for life in a Swiss sanitarium. Ilya Petrovich Tchaikovsky was dead,

Nicholas Rubinstein was dead.

Tchaikovsky sought for stability, and found it at Klin, a village convenient to both St. Petersburg and Moscow. Here was to be his home for the rest of his life.

Tchaikovsky's start toward house-furnishing was to buy a pair of horses which he afterward had great trouble in disposing of, and an English clock which would not go. Thereafter he left the arrangements to Alexis Safronov.

At the end of September, 1890, Tchaikovsky received a shattering blow in the form of a letter from Nadejda Filaretovna which wrote a full stop to their correspondence with sharp finality.

Apparently the letter has not been preserved; Tchaikovsky himself may have destroyed it. But from his reply it is clear that among other things Nadejda Filaretovna told him that financial reverses made it impossible to continue his pension; that she hoped she would not cease to exist for him now that she was poor; and that her letter ended with the words, "Do not forget, and think of me sometimes."

The blow was all the more stunning because unexpected. Tchaikovsky had had no reason to doubt her sincerity or solvency. It was not three months since she had sent him a considerable sum over and above his annuity, presumably to take care of some expenses connected with his house at Klin.

Tchaikovsky confessed to Jurgenson a panicky moment at the loss of his annuity. But he still had a life pension of three thousand rubles conferred by the Tsar two years before, his royalties and conducting fees, and he had only to say the word to go back to the conservatory. Moreover, his latest opera, *Pique-Dame*, was in rehearsal and its immediate and continuing success was to end financial cares.

He was in fact in a position to repay to Nadejda Filaretovna some of the money which she had advanced him. But he learned on reliable authority that her fortune was as sound as ever. So that part of her letter, at least, was false.

Tchaikovsky had reason to be grateful for past favors, but such is the frailty of human nature that he felt himself ill used. The relationship which had meant so much to him had been but the passing fancy of a rich woman. Her final letter, he told Modeste bitterly, had been "but an excuse to get rid of him at the first opportunity." He felt ashamed for having taken her money, although there seems to be no evidence of his offering to pay it back.

What caused the break? The official explanation of "illness" would not do, as Tchaikovsky pointed out to Pahulsky, by now Nadejda Filaretovna's son-in-law. Even if she were too ill to read his letters or answer them, she could certainly be told that her old friend Peter Ilyich was anxiously inquiring about her and wishing her a speedy recovery.

Pahulsky's replies were evasive. The mystery remains a mystery to this day.

Catherine Drinker Bowen believed Nadejda Filaretovna was suffering from a guilt-complex. Her eldest son, Vladimir, in the course of his activities as a wealthy sportsman had contracted a disease "against which medicine had then no weapon" and was wasting away before her eyes. The shock of this discovery made Nadejda Filaretovna realize she had been neglecting maternal duties for her romance-by-correspondence, which she thereupon broke off.

Herbert Weinstock, while dismissing Mrs. Bowen's *Beloved Friend* as a "fictionized and luridly colored story" which gave a false impression of the composer, picked up the Bowen guilt-complex theory in his own Tchaikovsky biography.

There are other possibilities. Nadejda Filaretovna might, belatedly, have found out about *"The."* Had the discovery come suddenly and unexpectedly, making clear in a flash the reason for Tchaikovsky's keeping her at a distance and for the failure of his marriage, the shock might have prompted her farewell letter.

She may have felt herself no longer needed. Tchaikovsky's fame by now was securely established. Or she may have felt his literary ardor to be cooling. As he became more and more enmeshed in rehearsals and concert tours, his letters to her contained frequent apologies for not writing oftener.

Or she may have been merely tired. She was sixty.

At any rate, Tchaikovsky obeyed her admonition. He was to think of her, not sometimes, but often; and would die with her name on his lips.

11

In APRIL, 1891, Tchaikovsky sailed for New York. He was to be one of the conductors at a festival celebrating the opening of Music Hall, now known as Carnegie Hall.

America is seen through Tchaikovsky's eyes in excerpts from his letters and diaries:

New York, April 27, 1891

We landed at 5 P.M. I was met by four very amiable gentlemen and a lady who took me straight to the Hotel Normandie. After all these people had gone, I began to walk up and down my rooms (I have two) and shed many tears.

After a bath, I dressed, dined against my inclination, and went for a stroll down Broadway. An extraordinary street! Houses of one and two stories alternate with some nine-storied buildings. Most original. I was struck with the number of Negro faces I saw. When I got back I began crying again, and slept like the dead, as I always do after tears. I awoke refreshed, but the tears are always in my eyes.

April 27, 1891

Mayer [head of the Knabe Piano Company] was my first visitor. The cordial friendliness of this pleasant German astonished and touched me. Then a reporter appeared, and I was very thankful for Mayer's presence. Many of his questions were very curious. Reno [Morris Reno, president of the Music Hall Company of New York, which had invited Tchaikovsky to conduct] next arrived and told me I was expected at the rehearsal. A magnificent building. We got to the rehearsal just at the end of Beethoven's Fifth Symphony. [Walter] Damrosch, who was conducting without his coat, appeared very pleasant. I had to answer the cordial greetings of the orchestra. Damrosch made a little speech. More ovations. I could only rehearse the first and third movements of the First Suite. The orchestra is excellent.

After the rehearsal Mayer took me up Broadway, helped me to buy a hat, presented me with a hundred cigarettes, and showed me the very interesting Hoffman [House] Bar. Damrosch took me to meet Carnegie, the possessor of 30,000,000 dollars, who is very like our dramatist Ostrovsky. Next to Moscow, which he visited two years ago, he admires the national songs of Scotland, which Damrosch played to him on a magnificent Steinway grand. He has a young and pretty wife.

After these visits I went with Hyde [Francis Hyde, president of the New York Philharmonic Society] and Damrosch to the Athletic Club and another, more serious in tone, like our English Club. We ordered drinks in the serious

club. I reached home about eleven o'clock.
Needless to say, I was worn out.

April 28

A messenger came to know if I wanted anything. These Americans strike me as very remarkable, especially after the impression the
Parisians left upon me; their politeness or ami-
ability to a stranger always savored of self-in-
terest; whereas in this country the honesty, sincerity, generosity, cordiality and readiness to
help you without any *arrière-pensée*, are very
pleasant.

At the great Opera House we heard an ora-
torio, "The Captivity," by the American composer Max Vogrich. Most wearisome. After this
I wanted to go home, but the dear Hydes carried me off to supper at Delmonico's. We ate
oysters with a sauce of small turtles (!!!) and
cheese. Champagne, and an iced peppermint
drink, supported my failing courage. They
brought me home at twelve o'clock. A telegram
from Botkin [of the Russian Embassy] sum-
moning me to Washington.

April 29

Reno gave a big dinner in my honor. The
table decorated with flowers. Each lady had also
a little picture of myself in a pretty frame. The
dinner began at half-past seven and was over at
eleven. I am not exaggerating when I say this,
for it is the custom here.

Opposite me sat Carnegie, the admirer of Moscow and the possessor of 40,000,000 dollars. His likeness to Ostrovsky is astonishing.

Tormented by the want of a smoke, and almost ill with over-eating, I determined about eleven o'clock to ask Mrs. Reno's permission to leave the table. Half an hour later we all took our leave.

April 30

I am convinced that I am ten times more famous in America than in Europe. Several of my works which are unknown even in Moscow are frequently played here. Is not that curious?

May 1

I breakfasted with Mayer, after which we went downtown. The houses downtown are simply colossal; I cannot understand how anyone can live on the thirteenth floor. Mayer and I went out on the roof of one such house. The view was splendid, but I felt quite giddy when I looked down into Broadway.

May 2

By 10:30 A.M. I was at the rehearsal in the Music Hall. It was held in the large hall, where several workmen were hammering, shouting and running hither and thither. The orchestra is placed across the whole breadth of the huge platform; consequently the sound is bad and unequal. This got on my nerves until, in my rage, I was several times on the point of making a scene, leaving everything in the lurch and running away. I played through the [Third] Suite and the [Coronation] March very carelessly, and stopped the Piano Concerto at the first movement, as the parts were in confusion and the musicians exhausted. The pianist, Adèle Aus-der-Ohe, came at five o'clock and played over the Concerto, which had gone so badly at rehearsal.

May 4

Reno told me some interesting facts about Aus-der-Ohe's American career. Four years ago she obtained an engagement at one of the symphony concerts to play a concerto by Liszt (she was one of his pupils) and came over without a penny in her pocket. Her playing took with the public. She was engaged everywhere, and was a complete success. During these four years she has toured all over America, and now possesses a capital of over $100,000. Such is America!

May 5

We drove to the Music Hall in a carriage filled to overflowing. The appearance of the hall, in the evening, lit up and crowded with people, was very fine and effective. The ceremony began with a speech by Reno (this had caused the poor fellow much perturbation all the day before). After this the National Anthem was sung. Then a clergyman made a very long and wearisome speech, in which he eulogized the founders of the hall, especially

Carnegie. The Leonore Symphony ["Leonore" Overture No. 3] was then beautifully rendered. Intermission. I went downstairs. Great excitement. I appeared, and was greeted with loud applause. The March went splendidly. Great success.

May 6

"Tchaikovsky is a man of ample proportions, with rather gray hair, well built, of a pleasing appearance, and about sixty years of age (!!!). He seemed rather nervous, and answered the applause with a number of stiff little bows. But as soon as he had taken up the baton he was quite master of himself." I read this today in the *Herald.* It annoys me that, not content with writing about my music, they must also write about my personal appearance.

May 7

I am fifty-one today. I feel very excited. The concert begins at 2 o'clock, with the Suite. This curious fright I suffer from is very strange. How many times have I already conducted the Suite, and it goes splendidly. Why this anxiety? I suffer horribly, and it gets worse and worse. I never remember feeling so anxious before. Perhaps it is because over here they pay so much attention to my outward appearance, and consequently my shyness is more noticeable. However that may be, after getting over some painful hours I stepped into the conductor's

desk, was received most enthusiastically, and
made a sensation—according to today's papers.

May 9

My concerto went magnificently, thanks to
Aus-der-Ohe's brilliant interpretation. The enthusiasm was far greater than anything I have
met with, even in Russia. I was recalled over
and over again; handkerchiefs were waved,
cheers resounded—in fact, it is easy to see that
I have taken the Americans by storm.

May 10

This has been a very heavy day. In the morning I was besieged by visitors. I went out at one
o'clock to call on the nihilist Starck-Stoleshni-
kov, but he lives so far away, and the heat was
so oppressive, that I gave it up.

Dining with Carnegie. During the evening
he expressed his liking for me in a very marked
manner. He embraced me (without kissing me;
men do not kiss over here), got on tiptoe and
stretched his hand up to indicate my greatness,
and finally made the whole company laugh by
imitating my conducting. This he did so
solemnly, so well, and so like me, that I myself was quite delighted.

Niagara Falls, May 12

I went to bed early. The roaring of the water-
fall is very audible in the stillness of the night.
I will not try to describe the beauties of the

falls; it is hard to find words for these things. On the Canadian side I was forced, in order not to be tortured by the thought of cowardice, to put on a very ugly costume, to go down under the falls in an elevator, walk through the tunnel, and finally stand right under the falls, which is very interesting but somewhat frightening.

Baltimore, May 15

The rehearsal was held on the stage of the Lyceum Theatre. The orchestra was small, only four first violins, but not bad. But the Third Suite was not to be thought of. It was decided to put the Serenade for Strings in its place. The orchestra did not know this work. The conductor [Victor Herbert] had not even played it through, although Reno had promised that this should be done. The Concerto, with Adèle Aus-der-Ohe, went very smoothly, but the Serenade needs many rehearsals. The orchestra was impatient. The young leader behaved in rather a tactless way, and made it too clearly evident that he thought it time to stop. It is true— this unhappy touring orchestra must be wearied by their constant traveling.

After the rehearsal I went home with Adèle Aus-der-Ohe, dressed and went immediately to the concert. I conducted in my frock-coat. Happily everything went very well, but there was little enthusiasm in comparison to New York.

Washington, May 16

Dinner at the Metropolitan Club, of which Botkin and his colleagues are members. The dinner was very gay, and I was so delighted to talk Russian once more, although this happiness was dimmed by the sad fact that my "s," "sch" and "tsch" are beginning to sound rather indistinct from age.

Philadelphia, May 18

I reached Philadelphia at three o'clock. Breakfasted downstairs. Went for a walk. The concert at eight P.M. The enormous theatre was filled to overflowing. After the concert, according to long-standing promise, I went to the club. The return journey to New York was very wearisome.

New York, May 20

At eight o'clock I was taken to the Composers Club. This is not a club of composers, as I first thought, but a musical union which arranges evenings devoted to the works of one composer. Yesterday was devoted to me, and the concert was held in the magnificent Metropolitan [Opera] House. I sat in the first row. They played the Quartet (E flat minor) and the Trio; some songs were very well sung, but the program was too long. I received an address; I answered briefly, in French; of course an ovation. One lady threw an exquisite bouquet of roses straight in my face. I had to speak to about a hundred people and distribute a hundred autographs. I reached home half dead with fatigue. As the steamer left at five o'clock in the morning, I had to go on board that night, so I dressed with all speed and packed while Reno and Mayer waited for me. Downstairs we drank two bottles of champagne, and drove off to the steamer. I said goodbye to my dear American friends and went straight to bed. I slept badly and heard all the noise when the steamer started at five o'clock. I came out of my cabin as we passed the Statue of Liberty.

12

NADEJDA FILARETOVNA's place as the recipient of Tchaikovsky's confidences had been taken to some extent by his nephew Bob Davidov.

Although Tchaikovsky often felt sorry for himself when he took pen in hand, an amusing letter exists in which he chaffs his nephew about his fondness for writers of the French "realistic" school. Tchaikovsky's description of his dinner hour in the manner of Zola reveals his literary tastes, his humor and his fluency at expressing himself in French:

> With a napkin carelessly attached to his collar, he sipped. No sound save the champing of enervated jaws. No light. A ray of the setting sun, penetrating as if by chance into the low, bare room, illuminated at times the sallow face of the master eating his soup, at times that of the valet, mustached, with Kalmuck features, stupid and cringing. *On devinaist un idiot servi par un idiot.* . . .

He was working, he told Bob, and found the going difficult. The new symphony which he was sketching would not come out right. He was making slow progress with his new ballet, *The Nutcracker*.

> Yes, the old fellow is getting worn out. Not only is his hair turning white and beginning to

fall, not only is he losing his teeth, not only
are his eyes dim, not only do his feet drag—
but he is growing less capable of accomplishing
anything. This ballet is far weaker than 'The
Sleeping Beauty'—no doubt about it.

Nevertheless he urged Jurgenson to order from
Paris a new instrument he had heard there, "something between a piano and a glockenspiel, with a
divinely beautiful tone." It was called a celesta,
and he was in a hurry to use it before Rimsky-
Korsakoff or Glazounov found out about it. He
did so, with good effect, in the "Dance of the
Sugar-Plum Fairy" from *The Nutcracker*.

Tchaikovsky had never done so much touring as
in the years 1891, 1892 and 1893. Although he de-
clined Morris Reno's invitation for a return visit
to America, he traveled incessantly over Europe.

He suffered dreadfully from homesickness. "I
have nothing to write about but fits of weeping,"
he wrote Modeste from Basel. But, back in Russia,
he was equally miserable. "Moscow is unbearable,
for there is scarcely a human being who does not
bother me with visits or invitations; or ask me to
look at an opera or songs; or try to get money out
of me in one way or another." He swore each
tour would be his last, but when one was finished
he was already planning the next.

On one of his tours he learned that his old
tutor, Fanny Dürbach, was living in her native
village of Montbéilard in eastern France. He visited
her there on New Year's Day, 1892.

"Mademoiselle Fanny came to the door," he

wrote his brother Nicolay, "and I knew her at once. She does not look her seventy years, and, curiously enough, has altered very little on the whole. The same high-colored complexion, and her hair is not very gray. She greeted me as though it had been only a year since we met—joyfully and tenderly, but quite simply.

"Naturally we started upon reminiscences, and she recalled a number of interesting details from our childhood. Then she showed me our copybooks, my exercises, your letters and mine, and—what was of the greatest interest to me—a few dear, kind letters from our mother. I cannot tell you what a strange and wonderful feeling came over me while listening to her recollections and looking over these letters and books. The past rose up so clearly before me that I seemed to inhale the air of Votkinsk and hear our mother's voice distinctly.

"I stayed with her from three to eight o'clock, without noticing how time went. I spent the whole of the next day in her society. In the evening I embraced Fanny when I took leave of her, and promised to return some day."

During most of 1892, Tchaikovsky worked whenever he had an opportunity at the stubborn new symphony. He could not shape the music to his liking, and in the autumn he destroyed the partially orchestrated score.

Then his muse returned. "I must tell you how happy I am about my work," he wrote to Bob. "Just as I was starting on my journey [to Paris in December, 1892] the idea came to me for a new symphony. The work will be entitled 'A Program

Symphony.' This program is penetrated by subjective sentiment. During my journey, while composing it in my mind, I frequently shed tears. Now that I am home again I have settled down to sketch out the work, and it goes with such ardor that in less than four days I have completed the first movement, while the rest of the symphony is clearly outlined in my head. You cannot imagine what joy I feel at the conviction that my day is not yet over, and that I may still accomplish much."

Work on the new symphony was interrupted in June when Tchaikovsky went to Cambridge University to receive the honorary degree of Doctor of Music, along with Saint-Saëns, Boïto, Max Bruch and Edvard Greig. The Latin eulogy which honored "Petrum Tchaikovsky" pointed out that his music, while cosmopolitan, revealed his fondness for the folk songs of his native land—"*patriae carmina popularia ante omnia dilexit.*" During the oration, in accordance with ancient custom, the undergraduates were permitted to hiss, cheer and crack jokes at the expense of the new doctors. When the laughter and noise had subsided, the Vice-Chancellor greeted Tchaikovsky as Doctor *in nomine Patris, et Filii et Spiritus Sancti.*

Tchaikovsky was amused and charmed by it all. "Cambridge," he wrote Jurgenson, "with its peculiar customs which retain much that is medieval, with its colleges that resemble monasteries, and its buildings recalling a remote past, made a very agreeable impression upon me."

Back at Klin, Tchaikovsky wrote Modeste: "I am up to my eyes in the symphony. The further I go, the more difficult the orchestration becomes. Twenty years ago I should have rushed it through without a second thought, and it would have come out all right. Now I am turning coward, and have lost my self-confidence. I have been sitting all day over two pages, yet they will not come out as I wish."

Nevertheless, the symphony made progress; exactly three weeks later, on August 24, 1893, Tchaikovsky wrote Jurgenson that he had not only completed the work, but had also made a four-hand piano arrangement of the score. "On my word of honor," Tchaikovsky added, "I have never felt such self-satisfaction, such pride, such happiness, as in the consciousness that I am really the creator of this beautiful work."

Rehearsals for the first performance began in St. Petersburg on October 22. Immediately Tchaikovsky made a paralyzing discovery. The members of the orchestra did not share his enthusiasm for his latest symphony. Tchaikovsky's spirits, as usual, were dampened. He prepared the symphony rapidly and carelessly, as if in a hurry to get the performance over with.

Although he stuck to his opinion that it was "the best thing I have ever composed or ever shall compose," he was unable to convince performers and public. At its première on October 28 the symphony fell rather flat. There was applause, but not the enthusiasm which usually greeted a new Tchaikovsky work.

"The morning after the concert," Modeste recalled, "I found my brother sitting at the break-

fast-table with the score of the symphony before
him. He had agreed to send it to Jurgenson that day
and could not decide on a title. He had abandoned
his original intention of calling it a 'program
symphony.' 'Why program,' he asked, 'since I do
not intend to explain what the program is?'

"I suggested 'Tragic Symphony,' but this did not
please him either. I left the room while Peter
Ilyich was still in a state of indecision. Suddenly
the word *Pathétique* occurred to me, and I returned to suggest it. I remember, as though it were
yesterday, how my brother exclaimed: 'Bravo,
Modeste, splendid! *Pathétique!*' Then and there,
in my presence, he added to the score the title by
which the symphony has always been known."

Eight days later, Tchaikovsky was dead. Although
he had appeared to be in good health, it was the
cholera season, and he had drunk a glass of water
which had not been boiled. Soon he was delirious,
calling out Nadejda Filaretovna's name in a re-
proachful tone. A priest was summoned, but could
not administer the Sacraments; Tchaikovsky was already unconscious.

"At three o'clock on the morning of November 6,"
wrote Modeste, "Tchaikovsky passed away in the
presence of his brothers Nikolay and Modeste, his
nephews Count Litke, Baron Büxhovden and Vladimir Davidov, the three doctors and his faithful servant Alexis Safronov. At the last moment an indescribable look of clear recognition lit up his face
—a gleam which only died away with his last
breath."

EXPLANATION OF LISTINGS

THE COMPOSITIONS of Tchaikovsky are listed in four categories—orchestral, piano and chamber music, vocal (including opera) and ballet music.

Under the names of the various composers of the "Five," their works are listed alphabetically.

In the case of certain pieces which have been recorded to the saturation point, only those recordings are listed which have features of special interest. *Le mieux* being *l'ennemi du bien*, there seemed no point in including as a matter of encyclopedic completeness poorly-performed or poorly-recorded versions of works readily available on other and better disks.

Non-listing, of course, may also indicate that a recording appeared after the manuscript went to press.

The quality of the recordings may be assumed to be adequate or better unless otherwise stated.

Listings are in approximate order of merit, although in many instances two or more existing performances possessed so many admirable features as to make selection difficult. Generally speaking, however, the nearer a recording stands to the head of the list, the more highly it is thought of.

All recordings unless otherwise noted are single 12-inch disks, monaurally recorded. As this was being written, stereophonic disks were just beginning to come on the market in commercial quantity.

What about stereo? Will it make existing LP libraries obsolete as rapidly and thoroughly as LP annihilated 78 rpm?

At present it is a little early to tell. There is widespread interest in stereo, and the steady stream of new disks would appear to indicate that those already issued have found a ready market.

Stereo, however, is still evolving, and developing "bugs" analogous to those of the early days of LP. Some of the stereo disks offer an exciting new dimension in music listening. Some of them are terrible.

The collector might do well not to junk his monaural library just yet. Certain disks of great musical and historic interest—those of Toscanini and Koussevitzky, for example—were recorded monaurally, hence cannot be transferred to stereo as readily as were 78's to LP.

The same point is stressed by record-makers, including those who have gone to stereo. They assure the purchaser he can buy monaural disks "without fear of future obsolescence."

Whether monaural disks will give "brilliant results" when played on stereophonic equipment is a point which is, at the moment, moot. Some say they will; others maintain there is no such thing as "compatibility" and that stereophonic players merely increase the noise level of monaural disks.

Since a stereo system has two of almost everything else, if room can be found for two tone-arms, one equipped with a monaural and the other with a stereo cartridge, this can be recommended as a very satisfactory solution of the "compatibility" problem.

BALLET MUSIC

A THOROUGHGOING Russian, Tchaikovsky shared the national passion for ballet and welcomed every opportunity to compose for this medium. He did not object to following closely the choreographic outlines of the great Marius Petipa and supplied music exactly as specified.

Petipa's outline for *The Nutcracker* called for: "Soft music, 64 bars—The tree is lighted. Sparkling music, 8 bars—The children enter. Animated and joyous music, 24 bars—Moment of surprise and admiration, a few bars tremolo—A march, 64 bars," and so on, bar by bar, to the end of the piece.

One would think the composer would have felt himself in a sort of straitjacket because of this confining synopsis. But Tchaikovsky, fretting no more than Wordsworth's nuns at their convent's narrow room, turned out the music to the required measurements, and in the process created three of the most brilliant scores ever composed for dancing.

AURORA'S WEDDING

This small-scale ballet extracted from *The Sleeping Beauty*, is familiar to ballet-goers everywhere. The Stokowski performance offers brilliant orchestral playing and lifelike recorded sound, but with Stokowskian peculiarities of pace and accent.

—Leopold Stokowski and his Symphony Orchestra. RCA Victor lm-1774.

The Nutcracker, Op. 71.

When Tchaikovsky's *Nutcracker* had its first performance, in December, 1892, even the composer found it "a little boring, despite the magnificence of its stage setting."

This is a judgment with which posterity, on the whole, has agreed. What keeps the work alive is the first of the two orchestral suites which the composer extracted from it.

For this reason, many listeners may prefer briefer versions to the full-length work. *The Nutcracker* is *in toto* a lot of Nutcracker. For those who will settle for nothing less, the Dorati performance is outstanding. As musical performance, and as recorded sound, it is one of the best of the Minneapolis recordings.

—Minneapolis Symphony Orchestra, Antal Dorati, cond. Two 12-in. Mercury ol-2-101.
—Philharmonic Symphony Orchestra of London, Artur Rodzinski, cond. Two 12-in. Westminster opw-1205.
—Symphony Orchestra of Radio Berlin, Otto Dobrindt, cond. Two 12-in. Urania ur-237.

Nutcracker Suite No. 1, Op. 71A

Among recordings of the Suite, those by Fistoulari and Rodzinski have the merit of being paired with the rarely-heard Suite No. 2, in addition to their excellence as interpretations of the music. The Fistoulari version has somewhat the best of it;

the experienced hand of the ballet pit-orchestra conductor is clearly in evidence.

—Paris Conservatory Orchestra, Anatole Fistoulari,
cond. LONDON LL-441 (with *Suite No. 2*)
—Philharmonic Symphony Orchestra of London,
Artur Rodzinski, cond. WESTMINSTER LAB-7042
(with *Suite No. 2*)
—Leopold Stokowski and his Symphony Orchestra.
RCA VICTOR LM-9023 (with Debussy: *Children's
Corner*)
—Philharmonia Orchestra, Herbert von Karajan,
cond. ANGEL 35004 (with Handel-Harty: *Water
Music*)
—NBC Symphony Orchestra, Arturo Toscanini,
cond. RCA VICTOR LM-1986 (with Waldteufel:
Skaters Waltz; Rossini: *"William Tell" Overture*)
—Philadelphia Orchestra, Eugene Ormandy, cond.
COLUMBIA ML-4729 (with *Sleeping Beauty* ex-
cerpts)
—Royal Philharmonic Orchestra, Sir Thomas
Beecham, cond. COLUMBIA ML-5171 (with
Chabrier: *España*; Ponchielli: *Dance of the Hours,
from "La Gioconda"*; Suppé: *Morning, Noon and
Night in Vienna*)

THE SLEEPING BEAUTY, OP. 66
Royalty was on hand when *The Sleeping Beauty* had
its first performance, on January 14, 1890, in a St.
Petersburg production costing eighty thousand
rubles. "Very charming!" was the comment of
Alexander III.

"His Majesty treated me in a most offhand manner," Tchaikovsky noted in his diary. "Well, God be with him."

If Alexander III was insensitive to the beauty of the work, as the ever-touchy composer supposed, few others were. In Russia *The Sleeping Beauty* won immense popularity, which continues to this day. Outside Russia a full-length performance is somewhat more rare, although there are excerpts which are universally familiar. There seems to be little dissent from the proposition that, aside from being absolutely enchanting music, *The Sleeping Beauty* is one of the greatest scores for dancing ever composed.

Irving's recording evokes the charm of a Sadler's Wells performance; one can almost picture Fonteyn *et al.* in the wings awaiting their cues. Fistoulari leads a graceful, poised performance of the work. Dorati's reading, while more energetic than expressive, is the most complete of the three.

—Royal Opera House Orchestra, Robert Irving, cond. Two 12-in. RCA Victor lm-6034.

—Paris Conservatory Orchestra, Anatole Fistoulari, cond. Two 12-in. London ll-636/7.

—Minneapolis Symphony Orchestra, Antal Dorati, cond. Three 12-in. Mercury ol-3-103.

Sleeping Beauty Excerpts

—Leopold Stokowski and his Symphony Orchestra. RCA Victor lm-1010.

—London Symphony Orchestra, Pierre Monteux, cond. RCA Victor lm-2177.

—Philharmonia Orchestra, Herbert von Karajan, cond. Angel 35006.

SWAN LAKE, OP. 20

Swan Lake, brought out in 1877, was the first of Tchaikovsky's great scores for dancing which were to add virtually a new dimension to ballet.

Before Tchaikovsky, few composers of the first rank had concerned themselves with ballet. Beethoven, it is true, had composed *The Creatures of Prometheus,* of which only the overture is performed today. That the ballet was less than a triumph may be inferred from Beethoven's laconic statement: "I have written a ballet, in which, however, the ballet master has not made the best of his part."

Ballet of course had been *de rigeur* in opera since the seventeenth century. Otherwise it was the domain of minor tunesmiths who turned out danceable but not very distinguished music. One of the best productions of this school, Adolphe Adam's *Gisèlle* score, still holds the stage, after a fashion, today. Tchaikovsky's great scores for dancing played an important part in ridding the ballet stage of musical claptrap. Having relished a work of full symphonic, dimensions, balletomanes in future would be less willing to settle for Drigo.

Full-length performances of *Swan Lake* have been highlights of recent Sadler's Wells visits to this country. Excerpts are in the repertory of virtually every company.

Swan Lake, Tchaikovsky's first venture into ballet, in the theatre just escapes tedium. For many listeners the music is less interesting, out of its ballet context, than either *The Sleeping Beauty* or *The Nutcracker.*

The "full-length" recordings by Dorati and Fistoulari raise the question of how complete is complete. Fistoulari's London version is a third shorter, and accordingly a third less expensive, than Dorati's. While the omitted music is no great loss, ballet-goers might find it interesting to hear those portions of the score which are left out in theatre performance.

Musically the Fistoulari version is preferable. It is a deft, light-fingered performance, pulsating with dancing rhythms which set the listener to visualizing choreographic patterns. Dorati leads the work in an energetic, muscular fashion which would be more appropriate for "Ein Heldenleben." Somewhat more pedestrian is the reading under Krombholc.

—London Symphony Orchestra, Anatole Fistoulari, cond. Two 12-in. LONDON LL-565/6.

—Minneapolis Symphony Orchestra, Antal Dorati, cond. Three 12-in. MERCURY OL-3-102.

—Prague National Theatre Orchestra, Jaroslav Krombholc, cond. Two 12-in. URANIA UR-605.

SWAN LAKE EXCERPTS

—London Symphony Orchestra, Anatole Fistoulari, cond. LONDON LL-1768.

—NBC Symphony Orchestra, Leopold Stokowski, cond. RCA VICTOR LM-1894.

—Philadelphia Orchestra, Eugene Ormandy, cond. COLUMBIA ML-5201.

—Philharmonic Orchestra, Herbert von Karajan, cond. ANGEL 35006 (with *Sleeping Beauty excerpts*)

—Covent Garden Orchestra, Jean Morel, cond. RCA VICTOR LM-2227.

ORCHESTRAL WORKS

TCHAIKOVSKY'S FIRST and great love was the orchestra. From the beginning of his career he was fascinated by its immense range and its wide variety of potential dynamics and tone colors. And, it should not be forgotten, the time spanned by Tchaikovsky's career was a period of exciting orchestral development. We take our splendid present-day orchestras so for granted that it requires an effort of imagination to picture how bad orchestral playing must have been in the early ninteenth century.

Domenico, the younger Scarlatti, wrote that he detested the woodwinds, because they always played out of tune. C. P. E. Bach, writing in the latter half of the eighteenth century, predicted that the *maestro al cembalo*, playing a harpsichord or piano, would always be necessary in orchestral performance; otherwise it would be impossible to keep the players together. A surviving tradition of Mozart is that, aside from the fine Mannheim Orchestra, players of his time found it difficult to play his allegros fast enough to suit him.

Around 1850, technical improvements such as the Boehm system of keys for woodwinds and valves for horns and trumpets began to raise standards of orchestral playing and to make new tonal resources available to composers. The latter seized on these new sound effects with avidity, none more so than Tchaikovsky.

But whereas some composers (Bruckner, for a particularly turgid example) went hog-wild in piling up tonal masses, Tchaikovsky scored with restraint. A big Bruckner *tutti* on thirty or more staves is merely a vast, muddy tonal blur. The marvel of Tchaikovsky's orchestra, on the other hand, is its lightness and transparency. As musicians put it, "everything sounds." If an instrument is in the ensemble, it has a reason for being there, and makes its presence felt.

Tchaikovsky was considerate of instrumentalists, too, writing almost invariably in an instrument's best register and in a way that showed it to advantage. A French horn player of long experience was once asked why almost nobody bobbles the horn passage in the slow movement of the Fifth Symphony. After mentally executing the passage, the veteran replied: "Oh, hell, I don't know—it just lays nice."

Tchaikovsky's weakness as a symphonist was in the manipulation of sonata form, a shortcoming of which no one was more aware than himself. In this respect he was to some extent the child of his time. The elaborate, highly artificial (in the sense that a formal garden is artificial) sonata form was a product of the Age of Reason; whereas Tchaikovsky's milieu was *Strum und Drang* and belated Russian Byronism. It was the Age of Romanticism in the arts, of the Gothic revival in architecture. Few of his contemporaries felt so utterly at home as Brahms did in sonata form. Tchaikovsky was at his most Tchaikovskyan when writing imaginative program music, brilliant display-pieces for orchestra.

The concertos put performers on their mettle. Whereas the Mendelssohn Violin Concerto, despite its brilliance, is relatively easy and among the first concertos assigned to conservatory students. Tchaikovsky's Violin Concerto is every bit as difficult as it sounds. So are the piano concertos and other works for solo instruments and orchestra. Generations of performers and listeners, however, have concluded the results to be well worth the trouble.

CAPRICCIO ITALIEN, OP. 45

At the end of 1879 Tchaikovsky was in Rome, living next door to the barracks of the Royal Cuirassiers. Every evening he heard the bugler blowing the fanfare which figures in the "Capriccio Italien." It appears to be a fragment of "Tattoo," an ancient call said to have been used by Wallenstein's armies in the Thirty Years' War. Some authorities say the United States Army designation is a corruption of "tap-zu," meaning the taps were shut and the night's beer-drinking at an end.

"The Carnival of Venice" and other Italian tunes are given a distinctly Russian cast by Tchaikovsky's scoring and harmonization. Galliera's performance with the Philharmonia is crisp, with brilliantly life-like sound. Fiedler, too, has a deft touch. The Collins and Schuricht performances are workmanlike, the Beecham a trifle stodgy. Moments of rough playing mar the Philadelphia performance, and Scherchen is a little heavy-handed.

—Philharmonia Orchestra, Alceo Galliera, cond. ANGEL 35047 (with Liszt: *Les Préludes*)

—Boston Pops Orchestra, Arthur Fiedler, cond. RCA VICTOR LM-1134 (with *"1812" Overture*)

—Paris Conservatory Orchestra, Carl Schuricht, cond. LONDON LL-640 (with *Theme and Variations from Suite No. 3*)

—London Symphony Orchestra, Anthony Collins, cond. LONDON LL-1441 (with *Francesca da Rimini*)

—Columbia Symphony Orchestra, Sir Thomas Beecham, cond. COLUMBIA ML-4287 (with Bizet: *"Carmen" Suite*)

—Philadelphia Orchestra, Eugene Ormandy, cond. COLUMBIA CL-707 (with Rimsky-Korsakoff: *Capriccio Espagnol, Flight of the Bumblebee, Dance of the Tumblers*)

—London Symphony Orchestra, Hermann Scherchen, cond. WESTMINSTER XWN-18598 (with Rimsky-Korsakoff: *Capriccio Espagnol*; Rossini: *"William Tell" Overture, "La Gazza Ladra" Overture*)

CONCERT FANTASY, FOR PIANO AND ORCHESTRA, OP. 56

This piece is all that remains of the projected Third Piano Concerto. Halfway through the concerto, Tchaikovsky became dissatisfied with it and recast it in its present form. Its Moscow première was a success, but Modeste Tchaikovsky noted that the cheers were for Taneyev's playing of the difficult piano part. Today the Concert Fantasy is played, if at all, as a historic curiosity. In Classic's recording a gifted young pianist named Tatiana Nikolayeva makes the most of the fantasy's opportunities for virtuoso display.

—Tatiana Nikolayeva, pianist; USSR State Orchestra, Kiril Kondrashin, cond. CLASSIC CE-7 (with Babajanian: *Heroic Ballad*)

CONCERTO NO. 1, IN B-FLAT MINOR, FOR PIANO, OP. 23

Since the B-flat Minor Concerto is a sure-fire item, the record companies have given it their undivided attention. As a result there are a number of recorded performances of such high merit that one is hard put to make a choice.

Of special interest is the recording by Van Cliburn, with Kiril Kondrashin conducting the Symphony of the Air. Aside from its merit as pianism in the grand manner, the disk is unique as a record of the greatest international triumph by a native pianist since the days of Gottschalk.

Ought one, then, to pass up the Toscanini-Horowitz recording? Although the recorded sound, like that of so many Toscanini-approved disks, is rather dry, it is a dazzling display of sheer virtuosity. Toscanini appears determined to prove that nobody can out-sprint the NBC Symphony; Horowitz, just the opposite.

And what about Rubinstein-Mitropoulos? As a recording this, too, is somewhat dated; but it is a stunning performance, with Rubinstein at the height of his powers, Mitropoulos a deft collaborator.

Gilels is all over the place, one listener favoring his performance with Reiner and the Chicago Symphony. The Period "showcase" disk, however, is a bargain to be remembered, offering at $1.98 Gilels in the Piano Concerto and Oistrakh in the Violin Concerto.

Pennario's is a straightforward, efficient performance, as are those of Malcuzynski, Uninsky, Serebriakov, Anda, Cherkassky, Katchen, and Wuehrer. Bachauer's powerful fingers were made to order for the heroics of the opening movement. Levant's, unfortunately, were not; and technical or stylistic limitations hamper Badura-Skoda, Bianca, Farnadi and De la Bruchollerie. Iturbi's feat of playing and conducting the Colonne Orchestra is hardly more than a tour de force; this is a work in which the conductor needs, so to speak, to drive with both hands on the wheel.

—Van Cliburn, pianist; Symphony of the Air, Kiril P. Kondrashin, cond. RCA VICTOR LM-2252

—Vladimir Horowitz, pianist; NBC Symphony, Arturo Toscanini, cond. RCA VICTOR LCT-1012

—Arthur Rubinstein, pianist; Minneapolis Symphony, Dimitri Mitropoulos, cond. RCA VICTOR LM-1028

—Emil Gilels, pianist; Chicago Symphony, Fritz Reiner, cond. RCA VICTOR LM-1969

—Gilels; Bolshoi Theatre Orchestra, Samuel Samosud, cond. BRUNO 14005 with Kabalevsky: *Concerto No. 3*)

—Gilels; Bolshoi Theatre Orchestra, Samuel Samosud, cond. PERIOD SHO-307 (with *Violin Concerto*)

—Leonard Pennario, pianist; Los Angeles Philharmonic, Erich Leinsdorf, cond. CAPITOL PAO-8417

—Witold Malcuzynski, pianist; Orchestre National de la Radiodiffusion Française, Nicolai Malko, cond. ANGEL 35543

—Alexander Uninsky, pianist; Hague Philharmonic, Willem van Otterloo, cond. EPIC 3LC-3010

—Pavel Serebriakov, pianist; Leningrad Philharmonic Orchestra, Eugene Mravinsky, cond. WESTMINSTER XWN-18179 (with Rubinstein: *Piano Concerto No. 4*)

—Geza Anda, pianist; Philharmonia Orchestra, Alceo Galliera, cond. ANGEL 35083 (with Delibes: *"Coppélia" Waltz*)

—Shura Cherkassky, pianist; Berlin Philharmonic, Ludwig, cond. DECCA 9605

—Julius Katchen, pianist; London Symphony, Gamba, cond. LONDON LL-1423 (with Liszt: *Hungarian Fantasia*)

—Friedrich Wuehrer, pianist; Vienna Pro Musica, Heinrich Hollreiser, cond. VOX PL-9000 (with Grieg: *Piano Concerto*)

—Gina Bachauer, pianist; New London Orchestra, Alec Sherman, cond. RCA VICTOR LM-1890

—Oscar Levant, pianist; Philadelphia Orchestra, Eugene Ormandy, cond. COLUMBIA CL-740 (with Grieg: *Piano Concerto*)

—Paul Badura-Skoda, pianist; Philharmonic Promenade Orchestra, Sir Adrian Boult, cond. WESTMINSTER XWN-18162

—Sondra Bianca, pianist; Hamburg Philharmonia, Hans-Jurgen Walther, cond. MGM E-3278 (with Grieg: *Piano Concerto*)

—Edith Farnadi, pianist; Vienna State Opera Orchestra, Hermann Scheren, cond. WESTMINSTER xwn-18578 (with Rachmaninoff: *Piano Concerto No. 2*)

—Monique de la Bruchollerie, pianist; Vienna Symphony, Rudolf Moralt, cond. Vox pl-10350 (with *Violin Concerto*)

—José Iturbi, pianist and conductor; Colonne Orchestra. Angel 35477

Concerto No. 2, in G, for Piano, Op. 44

The Second Piano Concerto has been occasionally performed in this country in recent seasons as the music for Balanchine's *Ballet Imperial.* Otherwise it has languished. This is regrettable, for the concerto is a sprightly work, and would be an agreeable change from the overworked B-flat Minor Concerto. Although the piano part is extremely difficult, there are performers who can play it. Perhaps the Second Concerto will have a renaissance some day.

In addition to its difficulty, the concerto has been hampered by its length. The standard abridgement, the *"Nouvelle édition revue et diminuée d'après les indications de l'auteur,"* was made by Tchaikovsky's pupil Alexander Siloti. Of the shorter versions, Cherkassky's is remarkable for the speed, accuracy and evenness of the rapid passages. A good word, too, should be said for the poised, assured performance of Benno Moiseiwitsch, though the sound is dated. Wuehrer performs competently; Farnadi is not up to the heroics of the solo part. Nikolayeva is a dexterous player, and the Classic Edition offers the complete original version; it is regrettable that the recorded sound has not more liveliness and sparkle.

—Shura Cherkassky, pianist; Berlin Philharmonic Orchestra, Richard Kraus, cond. DECCA DL-9916

—Benno Moiseiwitsch, pianist; Liverpool Philharmonic Orchestra, George Weldon, cond. RCA VICTOR LVT-1008 (with Rachmaninoff: *Concerto No. 1*)

—Friedrich Wuehrer, pianist; Vienna Pro Musica Orchestra, Heinrich Hollreiser, cond. VOX PL-9200 (with Scriabin: *Piano Concerto in F-sharp Minor*)

—Edith Farnadi, pianist; Vienna State Opera Orchestra, Hermann Scherchen, cond. WESTMINSTER XWN-18289 (with *Piano Concerto No. 1*)

—Tatiana Nikolayeva, pianist; USSR State Orchestra, Konstantine Anosov, cond. CLASSIC CE-3

"ROMEO AND JULIET," OVERTURE-FANTASY

Of the many recordings of this much-recorded work, the Toscanini is in a class by itself. The Maestro was fond of "Romeo and Juliet" as an orchestral display-piece. The recording is there to show that Toscanini's legendary conducting feats were not a figment of listeners' imaginations. The music pulsates with nervous energy from the first note to the last. Rapid passages are breath-taking; it seems incredible that an orchestra could be drilled and browbeaten into playing with such whip-lash precision.

Recorded sound, unfortunately, is gritty. A comparison with almost any recent recording will show how far the art of sound has progressed since this disk was made.

At the opposite extreme are the performances of

Scherchen and Eibenschütz. Phrases are dragged out at such interminable length as to make the music lifeless.

There is a happy medium between these extremes, happily occupied by Galliera, Cantelli, Ormandy and Munch. Judged both as interpretation and re-cording, Galliera's is perhaps best of the four.

The London Philharmonic plays indifferently for Van Beinum, with uncertain ensemble, ragged attacks and releases. The New York Philharmonic does little better for Bernstein. The Kostelanetz and Maazel performances are routine.

—Philharmonia Orchestra, Alceo Galliera, cond. ANGEL 35410 (with Strauss: *Death and Trans-figuration*)

—Philharmonia Orchestra, Guido Cantelli, cond. RCA VICTOR LM-1719 (with Mussorgsky-Ravel: *Pictures at an Exhibition*)

—Philadelphia Orchestra, Eugene Ormandy, cond. COLUMBIA ML-4997 (with *"1812" Overture, Marche Slave*)

—Boston Symphony Orchestra, Charles Munch, cond. RCA VICTOR LM-2043 (with *Francesca da Rimini*)

—London Symphony Orchestra, Hermann Scher-chen, cond. WESTMINSTER XWN-18283 (with *"1812" Overture, Marche Slave*)

—Leipzig Philharmonic Orchestra, José Eiben-schütz, cond. URANIA URLP-7158 (with *Francesca da Rimini*)

—London Philharmonic Orchestra, Eduard van Beinum, cond. LONDON LL-376 (with *Francesca da Rimini*)

—New York Philharmonic, Leonard Bernstein, cond. COLUMBIA ML-5182 (with Stravinsky: "*Firebird*" *Suite*)

—Andre Kostelanetz and his Orchestra. COLUMBIA CL-747 (with "*Sleeping Beauty*" *Waltz, Valse Mélancolique, Waltz from Serenade in C, Waltz Finale from "Nutcracker" Suite No. 2*)

—Berlin Philharmonic Orchestra, Lorin Maazel, cond. DECCA DL-9967 (with Prokofieff: "*Romeo and Juliet*")

—NBC Symphony Orchestra, Arturo Toscanini, cond. VICTOR LM-1019 (with Berlioz: "*Romeo and Juliet*," *Part II*)

CONCERTO, IN D, FOR VIOLIN, OP. 35

Being *de rigeur* for every concert virtuoso, the Violin Concerto has been recorded frequently, and most of the recordings are good. If one stands out, it is the Milstein-Munch version, for its combination of brilliant solo playing and well-balanced recorded sound. The Oistrakh performance is a frankly romantic and individualistic approach to the concerto, but in the matter of dexterity Mr. Oistrakh takes second place to nobody. The recorded orchestral sound is a bit dull.

Of the two Heifetz performances, that with the Chicago Symphony Orchestra is less successful. The soloist's playing sounds perfunctory, and without its usual blend of fire and precision. It sounds as if there had been an argument over tempi, which the violinist lost. The customary Heifetz élan is heard, however, in his performance with the Philharmonia Orchestra.

Erica Morini's performance has distinction, and Campoli's bravura playing of the rapid staccato passages of the first movement is a brilliant technical display. The fine playing of Zino Francescatti is marred by poor recorded balance; the solo violin overpowers the orchestra, and the delightful contrapuntal exchanges become monologues. In the Mischa Elman recording, the famous Elman tone does not wholly compensate for uncertain intonation and other technical flaws.

—Nathan Milstein, violinist; Boston Symphony Orchestra, Charles Munch, cond. RCA VICTOR LM-1760

—David Oistrakh, violinist; Saxon State Orchestra, Franz Konwitschny, cond. DECCA DL-9755

—Jascha Heifetz, violinist; Philharmonia Orchestra, Walter Susskind, cond. RCA VICTOR LM-1111

—Jascha Heifetz, violinist; Chicago Symphony Orchestra, Fritz Reiner, cond. RCA VICTOR LM-2129

—Erica Morini, violinist; London Philharmonic Orchestra, Artur Rodzinski, cond. WESTMINSTER XWN-18397

—Campoli, violinist; London Symphony Orchestra, Ataulfo Argenta, cond. LONDON LL-1647

—Zino Francescatti, violinist; New York Philharmonic, Dimitri Mitropoulos, cond. COLUMBIA ML-4965 (with Mendelssohn: *Violin Concerto*)

"1812" OVERTURE, OP. 49

This was a commissioned work, written for an 1880 ceremony and designed for performance in the square outside the Cathedral of the Savior in Moscow by a big orchestra, an auxiliary brass band, cannon and church bells. Tchaikovsky finished the score rapidly, confiding to Nadejda Filaretovna that "the Overture will be very loud and noisy, but I wrote it with little warmth or love; therefore it will probably have small artistic worth." Most musicians would heartily concur. Like the "Marche Slave," the "1812" Overture is full of the lurid melodrama and rhetorical flourishes which are "Tchaikovskyan" in a derogatory sense. Yet audiences have always loved it and probably always will.

The overture depicts in music the turning-back and eventual rout of the Napoleonic armies in 1812. The Russian landscape is depicted by means of Cossack and Nizhi-Novgorod folk songs. The French invaders are represented by a phrase from the "Marseillaise": "*Allons, enfants de la patrie.*" The "Marseillaise" is heard in the minor, and finally is eclipsed by the Czarist National Anthem. Bells ring, cannon boom and the hymn, "God Preserve Thy People," peals forth in token of victory.

Dorati's recording with the Minneapolis Symphony incorporates the sound of a revolutionary cannon at West Point, loaded with a double charge of black powder, and the bells of Harkness Memorial Tower at Yale. Fricsay's offers a novelty in the form of a "choral arrangement." Most of the others are of a sort calculated to make windows rattle.

—Minneapolis Symphony Orchestra, Antal Dorati, cond. MERCURY 50054 (with *Capriccio Italien*)
—RIAS Symphony Orchestra, Ferenc Fricsay, cond. DECCA DL-9738 (with Strauss: "*Radetzky*" *March*;

Verdi: *Overture to "La Forza del Destino," Prelude to "La Traviata"*; Smetana: *From Bohemia's
Woods and Fields*)

—Boston Pops Orchestra, Arthur Fiedler, cond.
RCA VICTOR LM-1134 (with *Capriccio Italien*)

—Philadelphia Orchestra, Eugene Ormandy, cond.
COLUMBIA ML-4997 (with *"Romeo and Juliet,"
Marche Slave*)

—Chicago Symphony Orchestra, Fritz Reiner, cond.
RCA VICTOR LM-1999 (with Liszt: *"Mephisto"
Waltz*; Weinberger: *Polka and Fugue from "Sch-
wanda"*; Smetana: *"Bartered Bride" Overture*;
Dvorak: *"Carnival" Overture*)

—Vienna Pro Musica Symphony, Jonel Perlea, cond.
VOX 8700 (with *Capriccio Italien, "Romeo and
Juliet," Marche Slave*)

—Vienna State Opera Orchestra, Mario Rossi,
cond. VANGUARD 484 (with *Capriccio Italien*; Rimsky-Korsakoff: *Capriccio Espagnol, "Russian
Easter" Overture*)

—London Symphony Orchestra, Hermann Scherchen, cond. WESTMINSTER XWN-18283 (with
"Romeo and Juliet," Marche Slave)

—Amsterdam Concertgebouw Orchestra, Edouard
van Kempen, cond. EPIC 3LC-3008 (with *"Romeo
and Juliet," Capriccio Italien*)

FRANCESCA DA RIMINI, OP. 32

When *Vakula the Smith* had gone into rehearsal
in 1876, Tchaikovsky was using what time he could
steal from the opera for a new work, inspired by
Doré's illustration of the passage in Dante's *In-*

ferno dealing with Paolo Malatesta and Francesca da Rimini.

"Francesca da Rimini" is an emotion-drenched work, in keeping with Dante. Does not the narrator fall in a swoon on hearing the sad tale? And he tells the shade of Francesca her sorrows have moved him to sad and pious tears: *"Francesca, i tuoi martiri/ a lagrimar mi fanno tristo e pio."* When to this is added the music of Tchaikovsky, restraint seems inappropriate.

The intensity of the score is well realized in Collins' performance, and the orchestral sound is lively. Munch, too, conducts with spirit. Jorda's interpretation ranks among the best. Ormandy's is a bit too genteel for this heart-on-the-sleeve work. Borsamsky's has great power, but with inferior recorded sound. Muffled orchestral sound also mars the otherwise excellent performance under Ivanov.

—London Symphony Orchestra, Anthony Collins, cond. LONDON LL-1441 (with *Capriccio Italien*)

—Boston Symphony Orchestra, Charles Munch, cond. RCA VICTOR LM-2043 (with *"Romeo and Juliet" Overture-Fantasy*)

—Paris Conservatory Orchestra, Enrique Jorda, cond. LONDON LL-376 (with *"Romeo and Juliet"*)

—Philadelphia Orchestra, Eugene Ormandy, cond. COLUMBIA ML-5242 (with Enesco: *Rumanian Rhapsody No. 1*)

—Leipzig Philharmonic Orchestra, Ernest Borsamsky, cond. URANIA URLP-7158 (with *"Romeo and Juliet"*)

—USSR State Symphony Orchestra, Konstantine

Ivanov, cond. WESTMINSTER xwn-18457 (with
Glinka: *Jota Aragonese, Summer Night in Madrid*
and *Symphony on Two Russian Themes*)

"HAMLET," OVERTURE-FANTASY, OP. 67

A free treatment, like "Romeo and Juliet," of
episodes from the Shakespeare play, Hamlet is less
successful than the earlier work. Tchaikovsky was
not the first or the last composer to find that
Shakespeare's philosophical tragedy does not lend
itself readily to musical treatment. (The overture-
fantasy should not be confused with incidental music
written three years later for a stage performance
of *Hamlet*). Both Fistoulari and Von Matacic labor
diligently to bring the music to life, the latter having
a bit the better of it in point of unity and coherence.

—Philharmonia Orchestra, Lovro von Matacic,
cond. ANGEL 35398 (with *"The Storm" Overture*;
Balakirev: *Overture on Russian Themes*)
—Philharmonia Orchestra, Anatole Fistoulari, cond.
MGM E-3002 (with *"Romeo and Juliet"*)

MANFRED, OP. 58

Although this work is in four movements and bears
the title "symphony," it has never been catalogued
with Tchaikovsky's other six symphonies and is
usually thought of as a sort of Lisztian "symphonic
poem."

The idea of a big symphonic work based on By-
ron's gloomy updating of the Faust legend was
broached by Balakirev in 1882, Tchaikovsky replied
that "Manfred" left him unmoved and anything
he wrote on that theme would therefore be worth-

less. But in a corner of his mind "Manfred" smoldered like an underground peat fire, bursting into flame three years later. It took such possession of him that he postponed *The Sorceress* and, "nervous and full of spleen all summer long," toiled at the big score until October 4. He had to show for his labors, he wrote Jurgenson, a work which "because of its unusual complexity and difficulty would be played only once in a decade."

The composer's forebodings were confirmed when "Manfred" had its first performance in Moscow on March 23, 1888. "Half successful," Tchaikovsky noted in his diary. "Still, an ovation."

The fact was that "Manfred" had got off the track. It was not quite a programmatic symphony in the manner of Berlioz' *Symphonie fantastique*, not quite a Lisztian tone poem, and not quite an orthodox symphony cast in the classical mold, though it made sporadic movements in all three directions.

Tchaikovsky himself, when the nerves and spleen of composition had worn off, saw clearly that this was the shortcoming of the piece. In a letter to the Grand Duke Constantine he outlined his intention to condense the four movements of "Manfred" into a tightly-wrought symphonic poem. But time pressed, *The Sorceress* would soon go into rehearsal and "Manfred" remained a work of "unusual complexity and difficulty."

It may have been that Arturo Toscanini found the work's complexity a stimulating challenge. Ordinarily no worshiper of Tchaikovsky, the Maestro was taken with "Manfred" and occasionally included it in his concert programs. Unfortunately his performance, while of great musical interest, is somewhat dry as recorded sound. Kletzki's performance with the Philharmonia is excellent, and the State Symphony of the USSR gives a good account of itself under Natan Rakhlin.

—Philharmonia Orchestra, Paul Kletzki, cond. ANGEL 35167
—NBC Symphony Orchestra, Arturo Toscanini, cond. RCA VICTOR LVT-1024
—USSR State Symphony Orchestra, Natan Rakhlin, cond. WESTMINSTER XWN-18536

MARCHE SLAVE, OP. 31

In September, 1876, Serbia, egged on by Russian Pan-Slavists, had been engaged three months in what eventually was called the Russo-Turkish War, and a Russian declaration of war was expected daily. In a fever of patriotic excitement, Tchaikovsky composed for a war-benefit concert what is perhaps the most enduring consequence of the Russo-Turkish War. Rating the recorded performances is difficult. As with a Sousa march, the main thing is to be loud and lively. Most measure up to this standard.

—Philadelphia Orchestra, Eugene Ormandy, cond. COLUMBIA ML-4997 (with "Romeo and Juliet," "1812" Overture)
—London Symphony Orchestra, Hermann Scherchen, cond. WESTMINSTER XWN-18283 (with "Romeo and Juliet," "1812" Overture)
—Boston Pops Orchestra, Arthur Fiedler, cond. RCA VICTOR LM-9027 (with Rimsky-Korsakoff: Capriccio Espagnol; Chopin: Les Sylphides; Mendelssohn: "Fingal's Cave" Overture)

—Philharmonia Orchestra, Wilhelm Schuechter, cond. MGM-e-3177 (with Brahms: *"Academic Festival" Overture*; Sibelius: *Romance in C*; Quilter: *Children's Overture*; Mussorgsky: *Hopak*; Humperdinck: *Witch's Ride*; Grieg: *March from "Sigurd Jorsalfar"*)

—Danish State Radio Orchestra, Eric Tuxen, cond. London ll-1313 (with Grieg: *Lyric Suite*; Sibelius: *Finlandia*; Liszt: *Hungarian Rhapsody No. 4*)

—Hollywood Bowl Symphony Orchestra, John Barnett, cond. Capital P-8296 (with Ponchielli: *Dance of the Hours*; Liszt: *Hungarian Rhapsody No. 2*; Saint-Saëns: *Danse Macabre*; Offenbach: *"Orpheus in the Underworld" Overture*)

—Vienna Pro Musica Symphony, Jonel Perlea, cond. Vox 8700 (with *Capriccio Italien*, *"1812" Overture*, *"Romeo and Juliet"*)

Serenade, in C Major, for Strings, Op. 48

The Serenade was written in the autumn of 1880, almost simultaneously with the "1812" Overture. Although the Waltz has been hackneyed nearly to death, other parts of the score are less shopworn and it is an excellent display-piece for the string section of an orchestra. Honors here go to the Philadelphians, but the Bostonians and Hamburgers, too, acquit themselves well. The Koussevitzky performance is chiefly of historical interest.

—Philadelphia Orchestra Strings, Eugene Ormandy, cond. Columbia ml-5187 (with Borodin: *Nocturne for String Orchestra*; Barber: *Adagio for Strings*; Vaughan Williams: *Fantasia on Greensleeves*)

—Boston Symphony Orchestra Strings, Charles Munch, cond. RCA VICTOR LM-2105 (with Barber: *Adagio for Strings*; Elgar: *Introduction and Allegro for Strings*)

—Northwest German Radio Orchestra of Hamburg, Hans Schmidt-Isserstedt, cond. DECCA DL-9517

—Boston Symphony Orchestra, Serge Koussevitzky, cond. RCA VICTOR LVT-1027

SERENADE MELANCOLIQUE, OP. 26

This charming minor work for violin and orchestra was written in 1875 at the request of the young violinst Leopold Auer. It is available in a fine recording made by Auer's brilliant pupil, Jascha Heifetz. In the Kurtz version the piece is rearranged for orchestra.

—Jascha Heifetz, violinist; Los Angeles Philharmonic Orchestra, Alfred Wallenstein, cond. RCA VICTOR LM-2027 (with Spohr: *Concerto in A Minor*; Rozsa: *Violin Concerto*)

—Columbia Symphony Orchestra, Efrem Kurtz, cond. COLUMBIA ML-4671 (with *Andante, from Symphony No. 1*; Shostakovitch: *Ballet Russe*)

OVERTURE, "THE STORM," OP. 76

This is the youthful work which earned Tchaikovsky a tongue-lashing *in absentia* from Anton Rubinstein on account of its elaborate instrumentation. And in fact Tchaikovsky did pile on orchestral tone color with a lavish hand. There are ominous drum-rolls, solemn trombones pianissimo made even more portentous by the addition of the tam-tam and other rhetorical flourishes. It is interesting to note, in this first orchestral score, how much of the essential Tchaikovsky is already present; also, despite occasional crudities, how genuine a flair for instrumentation is revealed. Lovro von Matacic conducts the work with gusto.

—Philharmonia Orchestra, Lovro von Matacic, cond. ANGEL 35398 (with *"Hamlet" Overture*; Balakirev: *Overture on Russian Themes*)

SUITE NO. 1, IN D, OP. 43

Tchaikovsky wrote this graceful work in 1879, just after completing the Fourth Symphony and the Violin Concerto, and before starting work on the Second Piano Concerto and "Capriccio Italien." At its first performance it was praised as a slight but agreeable composition. Today it is virtually forgotten. Tchaikovsky-lovers owe Mr. Mitropoulos a debt of gratitude for making the work available, since one is not likely to encounter it often in a lifetime of concert-going.

—New York Philharmonic, Dimitri Mitropoulos, cond. COLUMBIA ML-4966 (with Borodin: *Symphony No. 2*)

SUITE NO. 3, IN G, OP. 55

This is the work with which Tchaikovsky scored a triumph at his Carnegie Hall debut. Sir Adrian Boult's elegant performance with the Paris Conservatory Orchestra is preferable to the conscientious but hardly brilliant reading by Thomas Scherman and the Little Orchestra Society.

—Paris Conservatory Orchestra, Sir Adrian Boult cond. LONDON LL-1295

—Little Orchestra Society, Thomas Scherman cond.
  COLUMBIA ML-5256

SUITE NO. 4 IN G FOR ORCHESTRA, OP. 61 "MOZARTIANA"

Tchaikovsky's lifelong passion for Mozart led him
in 1887 to orchestrate four brief works by that composer in order to "bring them before a wider public."
He selected the Gigue in G, for piano, K. 574; the
Piano Minuet in D, K. 355; the Liszt transcription
of the Motet, *Ave, Verum Corpus*, K. 618; and the
Variations on *Unser dummer Pöbel*, K. 455. Liszt's
free piano transcription became even freer in Tchaikovsky's hands; and Mozart was touched up at other
points as well. This pleasant minor work receives
affectionate treatment from both Fistoulari and Van
Kempen.

—Philharmonia Orchestra of London, Anatole Fistoulari, cond. MGM E-3026 (with *"The Slippers"
  Suite*)
—Lamoureux Orchestra, Rudolf van Kempen, cond.
  EPIC LC-3213 (with *Serenade for Strings*)

SYMPHONY NO. 1 IN G, OP. 13 ("WINTER DREAMS")

This is the work which gave Tchaikovsky so much
trouble in his debut as a symphonist. Hearing this
charming, rather conventional piece, one would
never guess that it brought its composer to the verge
of a nervous breakdown. Both Swarowsky and Golovanov conduct the symphony in musicianly fashion,
but the Urania disk has more depth and spaciousness as recorded sound.

—Vienna Philharmusica Symphony, Hans Swarowsky, cond. URANIA 8008
—Bolshoi Symphony Orchestra, Nicolai Golovanov, cond. WESTMINSTER XWN-18224

SYMPHONY NO. 2 IN C MINOR, OP. 17 ("LITTLE RUSSIAN")

Tchaikovsky was thirty-two when he composed his Second Symphony in 1872. Although the work had a favorable reception, the composer was dissatisfied with it, and seven years later made a complete revision. This is the form in which the symphony is heard today. It derives its subtitle from its copious use of Little Russian (Ukrainian) folk melodies.

Of the available performances, Winograd's with the Hamburg Philharmonia is preferred for its fine evocation of the music and its superb clarity and depth as recorded sound. The Italian Giulini reveals an unexpected affinity for this very Russian Symphony, as does the Englishman Beecham. Swarowsky's performance is competent in every way. Solti's is refined to the point of slickness.

—Philharmonia Orchestra of Hamburg, Arthur Winagrad, cond. MGM E-3433 (with Mussorgsky: A *Night on Bald Mountain*)
—Philharmonia Orchestra, Carlo Maria Giulini, cond. ANGEL 35463 (with Mussorgsky: A *Night on Bald Mountain*)
—Royal Philharmonic Orchestra, Sir Thomas Beecham, cond. COLUMBIA ML-4872 (with *"Waltz of the Flowers," from "Nutcracker" Suite*)

—Vienna Philharmusica Symphony Orchestra, Hans
Swarowsky, cond. URANIA UX-109

—Paris Conservatory Orchestra, Georg Solti, cond.
LONDON LL-1507

SYMPHONY No. 3, IN D, OP. 29 ("POLISH")

When the Third Symphony had its first performance
at St. Petersburg in 1876, Cui found it to be not
without merit, but added that "we have the right to
expect more from Tchaikovsky."

Generations of music-lovers have, on the whole,
concurred, as demonstrated by the symphony's in-
frequent performance. It has Tchaikovskyan charm
—Tchaikovsky wrote few pages which were without
this quality—but it is rambling and diffuse and its
five movements have little structural relation to one
another. Its nickname is derived from the scurrying
Polonaise with which, for reasons not clearly apparent, Tchaikovsky chose to conclude the work. Altogether it is inferior to the Second, and hardly in
the same league with the Fourth Symphony.

This bit of minor but agreeable Tchaikovsky receives sympathetic treatment from Boult and the
London forces.

—London Philharmonic Orchestra, Sir Adrian
Boult cond. LONDON LL-1442

SYMPHONY No. 4 IN F MINOR, OP. 36

To name a "best" performance of this copiously-
recorded symphony is difficult. Certainly, from the
standpoint of superbly-balanced orchestral sound,
Angel's two performances by the Philharmonia Orchestra of London are second to none. Silvestri's

incisive reading highlights dramatic elements of the music more than does Von Karajan's. Ormandy's, offering the tonal splendors of the Philadelphia Orchestra, is solid and musicianly, without affectation or mannerisms. Argenta's is a deft, sure-handed reading striking for the clarity and transparency of its orchestral texture. The recording made by Kubelik during his Chicago tenure has stark, brooding intensity, and Mercury engineers achieved remarkable balance with a single Telefunken microphone suspended above the conductor's head.

The performances under Dorati, Fricsay and Furtwaengler are straightforward, Munch's somewhat episodic. Markevitch's interpretative flourishes do not always help the score, and both Scherchen and Rodzinski are a little heavy-handed. The old Koussevitzky disk, although dated as recorded sound, is musically as striking as ever.

Of special interest is the handsome Decca package offering the Fourth, Fifth and Sixth symphonies as performed by the Leningrad Philharmonic Orchestra under the direction of Eugene Mravinsky and Kurt Sanderling. This is calculated to satisfy the curiosity of listeners as to "how the Russians play Tchaikovsky." The answer is that they play it pretty much as everyone else does, a fact not surprising in light of the widespread concurrence on general standards of musicianship, and the virtually identical disciplines undergone by musicians, whether trained at the Moscow Conservatory, the Royal Academy or the Curtis Institute of Music.

The Decca recording leaves no doubt that the Leningrad Philharmonic is a first-rate symphonic ensemble, performing under resourceful and experienced conductors.

—Philharmonia Orchestra, Constantin Silvestri, cond. ANGEL 35565

—Philharmonia Orchestra, Herbert von Karajan, cond. ANGEL 35099

—Philadelphia Orchestra, Eugene Ormandy, cond. COLUMBIA ML-5074

—Orchestre de la Suisse Romande, Ataulfo Argenta, cond. LONDON LL-1275

—Chicago Symphony, Rafael Kubelik, cond. MERCURY 50003

—Amsterdam Concertgebouw Orchestra, Antal Dorati, cond. EPIC LC-3421

—RIAS Symphony, Ferenc Fricsay, cond. DECCA 9680

—Vienna Philharmonic, Wilhelm Furtwängler, cond. RCA VICTOR LVT-1018

—Boston Symphony Orchestra, Charles Munch, cond. RCA VICTOR LM-1953

—Orchestre National de la Radiodiffusion-Télévision Française, Igor Markevitch, cond. ANGEL 35446

—Vienna State Opera Orchestra, Hermann Scherchen, cond. WESTMINSTER XWN-18522

—Philharmonic Symphony Orchestra of London, Artur Rodzinski, cond. WESTMINSTER XWN-18541

—Boston Symphony Orchestra, Serge Koussevitsky, cond. RCA VICTOR LM-1008

—Leningrad Philharmonic Orchestra, Kurt Sanderling, cond. Three 12-in. DECCA DXE-142 (with: *Fifth and Sixth symphonies*)

SYMPHONY NO. 5 IN E MINOR, OP. 64

In many ways the Fifth is the most interesting of the Tchaikovsky symphonies. It is accessible at first hearing, but one must study the score to appreciate fully the skill and fluency with which the composer has manipulated his thematic materials. Its instrumentation is dark and rich-textured but never "thick"; Tchaikovsky was adept at keeping his orchestra in balance. The symphony is a work which, given half a chance, will make its mark in performance.

The performance by Steinberg and the Pittsburgh Symphony is exciting in every way. It is a forceful reading which follows closely the letter and the spirit of the composer's intentions, spacious and lifelike as recorded sound. Fricsay's performance with the Berlin Philharmonic is stirring, too, though not quite up to the Pittsburghers from the sound standpoint.

The Stokowski performance is interesting. It has the lush sound which is a Stokowski trademark, and the usual Stokowskian liberties are taken. Stokowski's habit of "sitting down on a phrase," as the saying goes, tends to make all the slow passages sound like the Prelude to *Tristan*. Everything sounds, however; all the inner voices come through. If one were following the work with score in hand, this recording would be especially valuable.

Eugene Ormandy and the Philadelphia Orchestra perform with restraint. If this is a shortcoming, it is almost the only one; it is first-class performance by a first-class orchestra. Much the same thing might be said of Karajan's and Silvestri's performances with the Philharmonia, and Rodzinski's with the Philharmonic of London. Solti's with the Paris Conservatory Orchestra is polished but a bit superficial; one feels he is too sophisticated, both as man and musician, to take so unabashedly romantic a work with complete seriousness.

The Russian viewpoint is offered by Mravinsky to good effect. Mitropoulos and the New York Philharmonic give a fine account of themselves except for a tendency to let things get out of hand when building up to a crescendo. The Koussevitzky record, aside from its considerable musical merit, is noteworthy as a memento of the conductor and orchestra who helped turn two generations of Americans into Tchaikovsky admirers.

—Pittsburgh Symphony Orchestra, William Steinberg, cond. CAPITOL P-8325
—Berlin Philharmonic Orchestra, Ferenc Fricsay, cond. DECCA DL-9519
—Leopold Stokowski and his Symphony Orchestra RCA VICTOR LM 1780
—Philadelphia Orchestra, Eugene Ormandy, cond. COLUMBIA ML-4400
—Philharmonic Symphony Orchestra of London, Artur Rodzinski, cond. WESTMINSTER XWN-18355
—Philharmonia Orchestra, Herbert von Karajan, cond. ANGEL 35055
—Philharmonia Orchestra, Constantin Silvestri, cond. ANGEL 35566
—Paris Conservatory Orchestra, Georg Solti, cond. LONDON LL-1506
—Leningrad Philharmonic Orchestra, Eugene Mra-

vinsky, cond. Three 12-in. DECCA DXE-142 (with
Fourth and Sixth symphonies)
—New York Philharmonic, Dimitri Mitropoulos,
cond. COLUMBIA ML-5075
—Boston Symphony Orchestra, Serge Koussevitzky,
cond. RCA VICTOR LM-1047

SYMPHONY NO. 6, IN B MINOR, OP. 74
("PATHÉTIQUE")

It is almost invariably the custom to play the rapid
passages of the "Pathétique" too fast; or, rather—
since tempi are relative, not absolute, and matters
of taste and opinion—at a speed at which it is impossible for the musicians to articulate the notes.
Even the fine players of a first-rate orchestra have
their speed limit. A fraction of a second is needed
for the string to "speak," the reed to crow; when this
is cut too fine the players are reduced to "hitting the
the high spots."

How this custom originated is not difficult to guess
upon listening to the Toscanini performance. And
even the NBC Symphony blurred a few passages in
getting up to the tempo exacted by the Maestro.
On the other hand, it is a very exciting performance.
Toscanini's conducting had superb rhythmic vitality.
The two-against-three effects which abound in the
work, and which must be done with absolute precision to make their effect, move with steady, effort-
less pulsation.

Hearing Silvestri immediately after the Toscanini,
or any other of the hotspur performances, gives an
effect like that of a slow-motion camera. His tempi
seem deliberate, even over-deliberate by comparison.

Then one observes that passages supposed unplayable are coming out clean; a rapid figure for the violins is an ascending scale, not a blur. There is a pace beyond which an orchestra cannot be driven through the "Pathétique," approximated in the Silvestri performance. Tonal balance is good, too; one can hear as much of the music in this as in any available recording.

Rodzinski's performance is on the deliberate side; Steinberg's has Toscaninian drive and intensity, with fine recorded sound. Ormandy's benefits from the superb sound of the Philadelphia Orchestra. The Ansermet reading is a competent, musicianly performance; Monteux's episodic and a little lethargic. Mitropoulos leads the work in a somewhat nervous, fussy performance. Markevitch, Mravinsky, Kleiber and Abendroth are overshadowed by the other excellent recordings available.

—Philharmonia Orchestra, Constantin Silvestri, cond. Angel 35487
—Philharmonic Symphony Orchestra of London, Artur Rodzinski, cond. Westminster xwn-18048
—Pittsburgh Symphony Orchestra, William Steinberg, cond. Capitol p-8272
—Philadelphia Orchestra, Eugene Ormandy, cond. Columbia ml-4544
—Orchestre de la Suisse Romande, Ernest Ansermet, cond. London ll-1633
—NBC Symphony Orchestra, Arturo Toscanini, cond. RCA Victor lm-1036
—Boston Symphony Orchestra, Pierre Monteux, cond. RCA Victor lm-1901

—New York Philharmonic, Dimitri Mitropoulos, cond. COLUMBIA ML-5235
—Paris Conservatory Orchestra, Erich Kleiber, cond. LONDON LL-920
—Leipzig Philharmonic Orchestra, Hermann Abendroth, cond. URANIA URLP-7147
—Leningrad Philharmonic Orchestra, Eugen Mravinsky, cond. DECCA DXE-142 (with *Fourth and Fifth symphonies*)
—Berlin Philharmonic Orchestra, Igor Markevitch, cond. DECCA DL-9811

THE TEMPEST, OP. 18

Another encounter with Shakespeare in which Tchaikovsky came off second best. Historically "The Tempest" is interesting as the work which first introduced Mme von Meck to Tchaikovsky's music. It is now neglected—unjustly, in the opinion of some Tchaikovsky admirers. Although Tchaikovsky did not rise to Shakespearean heights, the music has charm, spontaneity and, at times, a magical quality. Nevertheless, with conductors who know Tchaikovsky best, it's the "1812" Overture twenty to one. Fekete's performance, while perhaps not definitive either as performance or as recorded sound, is at least available.

—Vienna Symphony, Zoltan Fekete, cond. REMINGTON 55
—Philharmonia Orchestra, Anatole Fistoulari, cond. EMI-CAPITOL G-7119 (with Borodin: *Nocturne*; Glazounov: *Stenka Razin*)

Variations on a Rococo Theme for 'Cello and Orchestra, Op. 33

Tchaikovsky wrote these Variations, on a Mozartean theme of his own divising, for the 'cellist Wilhelm Karl Friedrich Fitzenhagen, his colleague at the Moscow Conservatory, in 1877. Like so many others of his work they reflect his lifelong adoration of Mozart. Solo 'cellists have eagerly seized on the Variations as a welcome addition to the limited repertory for their instrument, and they are heard with reasonable frequency in performance.

Fournier's superb tone, hair-true intonation and expressive playing make the Angel recording outstanding. Cassado's is a fine performance; Gendron and Navarra acquit themselves creditably.

—Pierre Fournier, 'cellist; Philharmonia Orchestra, Sir Malcolm Sargent, cond. ANGEL 35397 (with Schumann: 'Cello Concerto)

—Gaspar Cassado, 'cellist; Vienna Pro Musica Orchestra, Jonel Perlea, cond. Vox 9360 (with Dvořák: 'Cello Concerto)

—Maurice Gendron, 'cellist; Orchestre de la Suisse Romande, Ernest Ansermet, cond. LONDON LL-947 (with Schumann: 'Cello Concerto)

—André Navarra, 'cellist; London Symphony Orchestra, Richard Austin, cond. CAPITOL P-18012 (with Bloch: Schelomo)

PIANO AND CHAMBER
MUSIC WORKS

ALTHOUGH FLUENT enough at the piano to read through the score of *Carmen* (no mean feat if played accurately and up to tempo), Tchaikovsky was not a keyboard performer like Mozart, Beethoven, Liszt, Chopin or Brahms, or pianistically oriented like Schumann. The piano accordingly did not bulk large in his musical scheme of things. Aside from the big piano-with-orchestra works, the piano was for him a working tool rather than a vehicle of musical expression. His pianistic output was small and of little importance.

His chamber music output, too, was limited; but of some distinction. He seems not to have been greatly interested in chamber music, turning to it as a rule only when a suitable opera libretto or orchestral idea was not available. The opera house and concert hall were the places where he felt most at home and in which he most craved success. Nevertheless, when he occupied himself with chamber music, he did so with a will, and with often gratifying results.

ALBUM FOR THE YOUNG, OP. 39
This charming, Schumannesque work is agreeable if minor Tchaikovsky. It is heard in a deft, polished

139

performance by Miss Dorfmann, Westminster's artist is the veteran Russian pianist Alexander Goldenweiser, who studied at the Moscow Conservatory with Tchaikovsky's pupils Taneyev and Arensky. Pressler performs with spirit.

—Ania Dorfmann, pianist. RCA VICTOR LM-1856 (with *The Seasons*; Schumann: *Album for the Young*)
—Alexander Goldenweiser, pianist. WESTMINSTER XWN-18682 (with *Piano Sonata*)
—Menahem Pressler, pianist. MGM 3204 (with Mendelssohn: *Six Pieces*)

FIFTY RUSSIAN FOLK SONGS

One of Tchaikovsky's early projects, soon after joining the Moscow Conservatory faculty, was the arranging of these folk songs for piano four hands. Classic offers the collection in its "Music Minus One" series, with one piano part missing. The arrangements are of only moderate difficulty, and playing duets is good for developing rhythmic sense. Even mediocre pianists can have fun with this disk.

—Joseph Wolman, pianist, CLASSIC MMO-401

QUARTER NO. 1, IN D, OP. 11

With his debut as a writer of quartets, Tchaikovsky achieved a success equaled by few, including his own later works. The Andante Cantabile movement is perhaps the best-known item in the whole chamber music repertory. In view of this fact, one would expect the quartet to be almost as copiously recorded as the "1812" Overture. It seems incredible that only two recordings should be available, but such is the case. Perhaps the chamber music snobbery, which Herbert Weinstock justly assails, has touted players off the Quartet in D. It is heard in fluent, eloquent performance by the Oistrakh Quartet. The Hollywood Quartet's performance, while not quite matching the suavity of the Oistrakh group, has great vitality.

—Oistrakh Quartet. Colosseum 10190 (with *Serenade*)
—Hollywood Quartet. Capitol p-8187 (with Borodin: *Quartet No. 2*)

Quartet No. 2, in F, Op. 22

The almost universal neglect of this sprightly work, full of typical Tchaikovsky melodic invention, is difficult to understand. It is heard in fine and sympathetic performance by the Armenian Quartet.

—Armenian State String Quartet, Angel 35238

The Seasons, Op. 37A

This set of twelve piano pieces was written in 1875 for a music magazine in St. Petersburg. Tchaikovsky wrote them at the rate of one a month, forgetting about the project until reminded by his servant: "Peter Ilyich, isn't it time to mail that package to town?" By mailtime the package was always ready.

Neither the pianistic skill of Ania Dorfmann nor Morton Gould's clever orchestration quite obscures the fact that this music is minor Tchaikovsky. The two most popular months are June ("Barcarolle") and November ("Troikca").

—Ania Dorfmann, pianist. RCA Victor lm-1856
(with Schumann: *Album for the Young*)
—Morton Gould and his Orchestra. Columbia ml-
4487

Sonata, in C-sharp Minor, for Piano, Op. 80

Although bearing a late (posthumous) opus number
supplied by the publisher Jurgenson, the sonata was
actually written during Tchaikovsky's conservatory
days. Despite its obvious Schumannisms, it is a large-
scale work, dramatically conceived on big lines, and
thoroughly pianistic. Near-unanimous lack of interest in the sonata, however, is shown by pianists.
In Westminster's recording the Russian pianist
Samuel Feinberg, a pupil of Alexander Goldenweiser
(see note on "Album for the Young") plays with
style and authority.

—Samuel Feinberg, pianist. Westminster xwn-
18682 (with *Album for the Young*)

Souvenir de Florence, Op. 70

In 1890, while completing *Pique-Dame* and sketching the Fifth Symphony, Tchaikovsky visited Italy,
and the string sextet, "Souvenir de Florence," was
the result. The work was originally written for two
violins, two violas and two 'cellos. When he heard
the sextet performed, Tchaikovsky was unhappy. It
was thick-textured and did not "sound." The composer fussed over revisions but never got it entirely
to his, or others', liking.

When works stubbornly resist performance in
their original form—the Beethoven "Great Fugue,"

for example—recourse is sometimes had to a string orchestra. This expedient has been adopted for "Souvenir de Florence" by Arthur Winograd, 'cellist of the Juilliard Quartet.

—Arthur Winograd String Orchestra, Arthur Winograd cond. MGM E-3173

TRIO, IN A MINOR, OP. 50

Tchaikovsky once explained to Nadejda Filaretovna why he had written nothing for piano trio, a combination much favored by Austro-German composers. Tchaikovsky wrote that he did not greatly care for the sound of the piano, and especially disliked it as an equal partner with strings on account of the difficulty of achieving tonal balance.

Such is the perversity of human nature that soon thereafter he was hard at work on the A Minor Trio. The two available recordings are a lavish display of individual and collective virtuosity, the Rubinstein-Heifetz-Piatigorsky performance being possibly a bit the more lavish of the two.

—Artur Rubinstein, pianist; Jascha Heifetz, violinist; Gregory Piatigorsky, 'cellist. RCA VICTOR LM-1120
—Emil Gilels, pianist; Mstslav Rostropovich, 'cellist; Leonid Kogan, violinist; HERITAGE 1203

TWELVE PIECES OF MODERATE DIFFICULTY, OP. 40

Tchaikovsky's output of piano music tended toward salon-type potboilers. No. 12 of Op. 40 is called "Interrupted Reveries," and incorporates a song the composer heard daily under his window during an

1878 trip to Venice. Although these pieces seldom appear on recital programs, they are not without charm, especially as sympathetically performed by Reisenberg.

—Nadia Reisenberg, pianist. WESTMINSTER XWN-18005

VOCAL MUSIC

ALL HIS life Tchaikovsky had an unrequited affection for the operatic stage. His operas, even the moderately successful ones like *Pique-Dame* and *Eugene Onegin*, suffer from discursiveness. This appears to be a Russian national trait; it is the shortcoming of Borodin's *Prince Igor* and it makes the operas of Mussorgsky, Glinka and Rimsky-Korsakoff heavy going at many points. They, and Tchaikovsky, had not Verdi's keen eye for the dramatic main chance, building up ever-increasing tension until the final curtain. Tchaikovsky's successful operas succeed in spite of their librettos; the sheer beauty of the music sustains interest through dramatically arid stage situations.

Of Tchaikovsky's eighty-four songs, half a dozen, including the inescapable "None But the Lonely Heart," have retained a place in the repertory. His liturgical choruses are heard occasionally in the Protestant churches. In a class by itself is the "Liturgy of Saint John Chrysostom," serene music without a shadow.

EUGENE ONEGIN, OP. 24

Two excellent recordings of the opera are available, Westminster's by a Bolshoi Theatre cast and London's by the Belgrade National Opera. Westminster offers fine individual performances by tenor Sergei Lemeshev, as Lensky, and baritone Eugene Belov in the title role. The Bolshoi women's voices are, to one listener's ears, a bit shrill. London's is possibly a better-unified over-all performance. Both have so many merits as to make a choice difficult. The Period set, dubbed from an old 78-rpm recording, is not recommended.

—Soloists, chorus and orchestra of the Bolshoi Theatre, Boris Khaikin, cond. Three 12-in. WEST-MINSTER OPW-1303
—Soloists, chorus and orchestra of the Belgrade National Opera, Oscar Danon, cond. Three 12-in. LONDON A-4324
—"State Orchestra," A. Melik-Pashayev, cond. Three 12-in. PERIOD 507

MAZEPPA

Begun in somewhat desultory fashion during the spring and summer of 1881, *Mazeppa* was just barely not a failure when premièred in Moscow and St. Petersburg in 1884. Today, while infrequently heard outside Russia, its popularity there is exceeded only by *Pique-Dame* and *Eugene Onegin*.

The Bolshoi Theatre recording is now out of print, but a sufficiently determined Tchaikovskyan might turn up a set by canvassing record dealers.

—Soloists, chorus and orchestra of the Bolshoi Theatre, Vassily Nebolsin, cond. Three 12-in. CONCERT HALL SOCIETY CHS-1310

PIQUE-DAME, OP. 68

Pique-Dame ("The Queen of Spades") is Tchaikovsky's most successful opera. Its characters are well drawn and its dramatic situations are believable. The music is theatrically effective; occasionally, as in the scene between Lisa and Hermann on the banks of the Neva, rising to heights of almost Verdian intensity.

A well-staged *Pique-Dame* was a highlight of the New Opera Company's 1940 season in New York. Perhaps someone will get around to doing it again. In the meantime one can hear it on records. Best of the available recordings is London's. The Colosseum version is inferior as recorded sound. The abridged Urania German-language version was recorded from a Radio Berlin broadcast.

—Soloists, chorus and orchestra of the Belgrade National Opera. Four 12-in. LONDON A-4410
—Soloists, chorus and orchestra of the Bolshoi Theatre. Four 12-in. COLOSSEUM 130/3
—Soloists, chorus and orchestra of Radio Berlin. Two 12-in. URANIA URLP-207

"CHEREVICHKY" ("THE SLIPPERS") SUITE

Tchaikovsky's second attempt to write for the operatic stage resulted in *Vakoula, the Smith*, Op. 14. It was a failure, sharing the fault common in greater or less degree to all his operas. Tchaikovsky was not much interested in voices, hence incapable of writing a genuine "singers' opera." However, he believed in *Vakoula*, even if no one else did, and recast it as *Cherevichky*. It has also been called *Oxana's Caprices*. Under no name, in no country, has it held the stage. A suite drawn from the opera, incorporating the orchestral passages which are among the best things in the work, is admirably performed under Fistoulari.

—Philharmonia Orchestra of London, Anatole Fistoulari, cond. MGM E-3026 (with *Suite No. 4 "Mozartiana"*)

The Sorceress

This work, begun optimistically in January, 1885, followed a familiar pattern. Mounted with care after eighteen days of rehearsals on October 12, 1887, with magnificent sets and costumes and the best cast that could be scraped together, the opera earned its composer an ovation on opening night, but by November 29 was played to a half-empty house. Today it is moribund in Russia and extinct elsewhere. And in truth it is not a distinguished score aside from bright moments like the heroine's aria. "Where art thou, my beloved?" in Act IV. For the Tchaikovsky collector who has everything, an excellent Bolshoi Theatre performance is available.

—Soloists of the Bolshoi Theatre, State Radio Chorus, Moscow Philharmonic Orchestra, Samuel Samosud, cond. Four 12-in. WESTMINSTER OPW-1402

THE DIVINE LITURGY OF SAINT JOHN CHRYSOSTOM, OP. 41

Tchaikovsky, a lifelong churchman, was mildly scandalized by Nadejda Filaretovna's avowed agnosticism. Writing from Vienna in 1877, he told her: "The liturgy of John of Chrysostom is, I think, one of the greatest of artistic creations. If one follows our Orthodox service attentively, with full understanding of every rite and symbol, one cannot remain spiritually untouched."

Eleven years later Tchaikovsky set the Divine Liturgy to music, eliciting protests from Orthodox clergymen that the work was not meant to be a concert-hall divertissement. Interestingly, the note of melancholy so often found in Tchaikovsky's music is almost wholly absent from this sunny score. It is heard in an admirable performance by New York Russians.

—Cathedral Choir of the Holy Virgin Protection Cathedral, Nicholas Afonsky, cond. WESTMINSTER XWN-18727

The Five

BALAKIREV

Biographical Sketch

IN 1868 a St. Petersburg newspaper caricatured a meeting of the five composers known as the *Koochka,* or "Invincible Band."

Mily Balakirev was shown in Russian national costume, beating a drum; César Cui, as an artillery officer; A. P. Borodin, with a chemist's retort; Nikolay Rimsky-Korsakoff, as a crab; and, leading the procession, Modeste Mussorgsky as a strutting rooster.

Those who undertake to show their fellows the error of their ways must be prepared for a certain amount of chaffing. Somewhat bumptiously, the *Koochka* (a corruption of the Greek word for "clan" or "band") had flung down the gauntlet to the Western-oriented Conservatory group, announcing their intention of creating a school of "true Russian music." Public reaction, in the early stages at least, was somewhat skeptical.

The close association of the Five was brief. Like *Les six français* of the 1920's, members of the Five soon began to go their separate ways. The heyday of the *Koochka* was the early part of the 1860's. By 1873, *esprit de corps* had so diminished that Cui's hostile press notices were a major obstacle to performance of Mussorgsky's *Boris Godunov*.

In the early stages, the dynamic personality of Balakirev was the force which held the group together. Meetings of the *Koochka*, at which members performed their own works and discussed those of their fellows, took place regularly at Balakirev's apartment. Balakirev recognized Cui as almost his equal, by seniority and previous musical training. Chemist Borodin, Guardsman Mussorgsky and Sailor Rimsky-Korsakoff sat at the feet of Gamaliel. When Balakirev's influence waned, the end of the *Koochka* began.

Although no satisfactory biography of Balakirev exists, a little more is known of him than what Carl Van Vechten wrote: that he was brought up in the household of one Ulybyshev, a "music-critic," where he had access to a full-fledged symphony orchestra.

Even in Imperial Russia, "music critics" did not maintain private orchestras. Alexander Oulibicheff (to give his name its more familiar spelling)* owned a large estate near the ancient city of Nizhi-Novgorod. He was a Russian nobleman, an amateur violinist and music patron whose three-volume life

---

* All spellings of Russian names are phonetic approximations of the Cyrillic letters, which are descended from the Greek alphabet introduced into Russia by early missionaries of the Byzantine Church. "Balakirev" sometimes appears as "Balakiref" or "Balakirew." "Moussorgsky" is as correct as "Mussorgsky." Some years ago there was an unsuccessful attempt to replace "Tchaikovsky" and "Tschaikowsky" with "Chaikovsky." That is how most people pronounce it, but the idea did not catch on.

of Mozart (1844) was for a long time the definitive
work in its field.

From Karl Eiserich, the conductor of his orchestra, Oulibicheff heard of a wonderfully gifted boy,
Mily Balakirev, who was Eiserich's piano student.
Early in his teens, Balakirev joined the Oulibicheff
establishment, first as assistant conductor and rehearsal pianist, and eventually succeeding his
teacher as leader of the orchestra.

With the advantage of hindsight, it can be inferred what went on during the four or five years
in which Balakirev functioned at the Oulibicheff
concerts in addition to his regular academic studies.
The Oulibicheff music library was a good one, and
through it Balakirev became acquainted with the
orchestral works of Mozart, Beethoven, Mendelssohn, Hummel and others. One of the first
works which he helped to rehearse was the Mozart
Requiem. He heard and was enchanted by Chopin's
E Minor Piano Concerto and excerpts from Glinka's
A *Life for the Tsar*. He even composed a "Grand
Fantasy on Russian National Airs" bearing the
Italo-Latin inscription: *"Finis del prima parte Auctor
Milius Balakirev."*

Small wonder, then, that Balakirev was able to
impress other members of the *Koochka* with the
vastness of his musical experience. But his knowledge, while wide, appears to have been superficial.
His mind was not analytical; it does not seem to
have occurred to him that firmly-fixed basic principles underlie the apparently endless diversity of
music. According to eyewitnesses, he was a highly
efficient conductor; but we have Rimsky-Korsakoff's

testimony that Balakirev's acquaintance with the orchestra did not include detailed knowledge of orchestral instruments. One cannot imagine Balakirev, like Hans Richter, stopping a rehearsal and taking a player's instrument—any instrument—to demonstrate how the passage ought to be played.

When Balakirev had finished his high school curriculum, he was sent to the University of Kazan to study mathematics. Balakirev toyed with the idea of becoming a professional mathematician, keeping music as a side-line, always hoping against hope that he would be able to devote himself full-time to music.

Oulibicheff resolved the dilemma by taking the ninteen-year-old musician to St. Petersburg, where Balakirev made his debut as piano soloist in the Beethoven "Emperor" Concerto. It was a brilliant affair, attended by the Imperial family. Balakirev was presented to the Tsar. He might well have launched himself on a career as a solo pianist, but he did not enjoy playing in public. He supported himself by giving piano lessons—often as many as nine a day—and instruction in composition.

Rimsky-Korsakoff, who for reasons to be seen was a heavily-biased witness where Balakirev was concerned, nevertheless paid tribute to Balakirev's tremendous musical gift. Balakirev was an excellent pianist, a fluent sight reader and had a marvelous gift for improvisation. He memorized instantly music played for him and could remember, apparently, every bar of every composition he had ever heard.

Although Balakirev had had no formal training

in the technique of composition, this lack was compensated by his innate musicality and his phenomenal memory. For the solution of virtually any problem, Balakirev could recall a precedent in Haydn, Mozart or Beethoven.

It was this, said Rimsky-Korsakoff, that made Balakirev "a marvelous critic, especially a *technical* critic. He instantly felt every technical imperfection or error, he grasped a defect in form at once. Whenever I or other young men, later on, played him our essays at composition, he instantly caught all the defects of form, modulation and so on, and forthwith seating himself at the piano, he would improvise and show how the composition in question should be changed. Frequently entire passages in other people's works became his and not their putative authors' at all."

Cui and Mussorgsky were the first to join the Balakirev circle. With the addition of Rimsky-Korsakoff, in 1861, and Borodin the next year, the *Koochka* was complete.

In 1867 Balakirev made the unwise decision to become Director of the newly-founded Free School of Music in St. Petersburg. In its brief existence the school had done well from an artistic, badly from a financial point of view. Balakirev was not the man for balancing budgets, and showed little talent as an administrator. He had not the tact and flexibility which such a post requires.

The following year, when Anton Rubinstein resigned as conductor of the Russian Musical Society concerts, Balakirev was named his successor. By the end of his first season Balakirev had antagonized the Grand Duchess Elena Pavlovna, patroness of the concerts, had offended the players in the orchestra and was not on speaking terms with the board of directors. In the spring of 1869 he was compelled to resign.

"Things are very hard for poor Mily," Borodin wrote his wife at this time, "and yet I never saw him so buoyant and cheerful, so energetic and active. There's a true artist for you!"

But the "true artist" was not as cheerful as he seemed. In 1870 sheer financial desperation forced Balakirev to take a job at the freight station of the Warsaw Railroad in St. Petersburg.

Balakirev now began to withdraw from musical activity. He lost interest not only in other people's compositions, but in his own as well. A nervous breakdown, precipitated by the long series of crises he had undergone, left Balakirev an apathetic wraith of his former self. "I felt I was confronting a coffin," the critic V. V. Stassov wrote to Rimsky-Korsakoff, "and not the live, energetic, restless Balakirev we knew, so eager to peer into everything new, to question and press everyone he met. Now nothing interests him."

During this period Balakirev became deeply involved with a woman fortuneteller. Some of his friends believed the soothsayer was in love with Balakirev, a bachelor whom many women found appealing. For his part, Balakirev wanted to know the outcome of his feud with the Russian Musical Society. In the soothsayer's mirror, he told Rimsky-Korsakoff, he could see the Grand Duchess and the orchestra's board of directors. It was at this time that Borodin wrote: "I fear his mind is not quite in order."

From flirting with the powers of darkness, Balakirev turned to piety. He who had been a scoffer now had holy images in every room of his home. He attended church services daily. He had given up wearing furs, smoking and eating meat. His love for all living creatures was so great that if a noxious insect found its way into his room he would catch it with care and throw it out the window, wishing it "Godspeed."

Balakirev's situation improved when he was appointed "inspector of musical classes" at two St. Petersburg schools. No longer hard-pressed financially, he started seeing musical friends again, and resumed work on his compositions.

Despite his fluency in improvisation, Balakirev composed slowly and painfully, with many revisions. His opera *Tamara*, at which he had been working for years, was finally produced in 1882. Its great success was a factor in his appointment, the following year, as Director of the Court Chapel.

Balakirev was now able to indulge his taste for hospitality. As a host he had the peculiarity of dividing his guests into well-marked categories. Tuesday evenings were for musicians only, and no women were permitted. Even his visiting niece had to leave before 8 P.M. But a musician who called unexpectedly at another time found Balakirev entertaining a roomful of ladies. After introducing the musician all round Balakirev hustled him out, saying quite audibly: "You know that I am always glad to see you on *Tuesdays*."

A new *Koochka*, composed of Liapounov and other younger men, had begun to evolve out of Balakirev's Tuesday evenings. As for the original group, its relations with Balakirev were by now severely strained. The presence of Rimsky-Korsakoff, for example, on the staff of the Court Chapel was a source of embarrassment both to himself and Balakirev.

In 1890 Balakirev retired on a pension. He spent his last years composing his Second Symphony and his Piano Concerto (the final movement of the latter completed by Liapounov), conducting, preparing a new edition of Glinka's works, and organizing festivals in honor of Glinka and Chopin. He outlived all the others of the Five but Cui, dying after a lengthy illness in 1910.

ISLAMEY (ORIENTAL FANTASY)

Nizhi-Novgorod, Balakirev's boyhood home, was for centuries the eastern outpost of Muscovite Russia and a great East-West trade center. Balakirev as a boy must have seen the Asiatic caravans arrive and heard the playing of Eastern musicians in the streets of Nizhi-Novgorod. For that matter, Balakirev's Tartar features have been taken as evidence that his ancestry included an Asiatic strain.

All his life Balakirev was fascinated by Oriental themes, which he used most notably in "Islamey" and "Tamar." Both works, projected in the sixties, had their first public performance in 1882.

"Islamey" was composed for piano solo. The late Harold Bauer named it, and De Falla's "Nights in the Gardens of Spain," as the two most nearly unplayable works in the piano repertory. One pianist not daunted by the difficulties of the work is Alfred Brendel, who plays it with much vigor and conviction.

In Alfredo Casella's transcription, "Islamey" is a superb orchestral display-piece. Von Matacic shows himself to be a sympathetic interpreter, and the Philharmonia players offer a sparkling performance, on a disk which for Balakirev collectors has the further merit of being devoted entirely to that composer. Perlea's reading is competent but not especially remarkable.

—Alfred Brendel, pianist. Vox 9140 (with Mussorgsky: *Pictures at an Exhibition*; Stravinsky: *Petrouchka*)

—Julius Katchen, pianist. LONDON LD-9175 (with Liszt: *Hungarian Rhapsody No. 12*)

—Philharmonia Orchestra, Lovro von Matacic, cond. ANGEL 35291 (with *Tamar*; *Russia*)

—Bamberg Symphony Orchestra, Jonel Perlea, cond. Vox 10280 (with Liadov: *Baba Yaga*; *Eight Russian Folk Songs*; *Enchanted Lake*; *Kikimora*)

OVERTURE ON THREE RUSSIAN THEMES
This work, written in 1858, was built on three Russian folk songs, one of which, "In the Meadow Stood a Birch Tree," turned up almost twenty years later in the final movement of Tchaikovsky's Fourth Symphony. It is performed with enthusiasm by Von Matacic and the Philharmonia.

—Philharmonia Orchestra, Lovro von Matacic, cond.

ANGEL 35398 (with Tchaikovsky: *"Hamlet" Overture, "The Storm"*)

RUSSIA

This symphonic poem, sometimes titled "Russ" (the old Slavonic spelling of "Russia") was written in 1862 to commemorate the thousanth anniversary of the founding of the Russian nation. It is built on three folk tunes, each symbolizing a particular period of Russian history. The finale is a prayer for Russia's future.

The performance by Ivanov and the USSR State Orchestra has impressive power, breath and grandeur, surpassing in this respect the excellent Philharmonia performance under Von Matacic.

—USSR State Symphony Orchestra, Konstantin Ivanov, cond. WESTMINSTER XWN-18120 (with Rimsky-Korsakoff: *Sadko, Sea Episode; Fantasy on Russian Themes*)

—Philharmonia Orchestra, Lovro von Matacic, cond. ANGEL 35291 (with *Tamar; Islamey*)

SYMPHONY No. 1 IN C

Balakirev wrote two symphonies, in C and D Minor, neither of which has been able to hold a permanent place in the repertory. The Symphony in C, although uneven, is colorful, folk-oriented and spiced with exoticisms, like other works of this gifted, erratic and highly original composer.

Sir Thomas Beecham, a vigorous champion of musical lost causes, who almost singlehandedly saved Delius from oblivion, has from time to time interested himself in the neglected works of Russian composers (see comment on Tchaikovsky: Second Symphony). If a recording were able to rescue the Balakirev symphony from limbo, the zealous, carefully-detailed performance under Sir Thomas would do it.

—Royal Philharmonic Orchestra, Sir Thomas Beecham, cond. ANGEL 35399

TAMAR

This work was originally intended as a sort of orchestral companion-piece for "Islamey." It is characterized by brilliant Oriental flavor of the sort dear to most of the Five.

Fistoulari leads the work in a sumptuously-recorded, lively performance in which its Russianisms are well delineated. Von Matacic's reading, though less spectacular, leaves no doubt of his affinity for the Balakirev idiom. Ansermet's reading is crisp and precisely detailed; Perlea's is a competent, craftsmanly performance.

—London Symphony Orchestra, Anatole Fistoulari, cond. MGM 3076 (with Rimsky-Korsakoff: *"Ivan the Terrible"* Suite)
—Philharmonia Orchestra, Lovro von Matacic, cond. ANGEL 35291 (with *Islamey; Russia*)
—Orchestre de la Suisse Romande, Ernest Ansermet, cond. LONDON LL-1068 (with Liadov: *Baba Yaga; Eight Russian Folk Songs; Kikimora*)
—Bamberg Symphony Orchestra, Jonel Perlea, cond. Vox 9530 (with Borodin: *Polovtsian Dances;* Cui: *Tarantella;* Mussorgsky: A *Night on Bald Mountain*)

BORODIN

Biographical Sketch

ALEXANDER PORFIROVICH BORODIN, born in St. Petersburg on November 12, 1833, was the illegitimate son of the sixty-one-year-old Prince Luke Ghedeanov and twenty-four-year-old Eudoxia Kleineke. For propriety's sake he was registered as the son of one of his father's serfs, Porfiry Borodin.

He was brought up by his mother in a comfortable household where music-making was taken for granted. Young Borodin's talent showed itself early. At nine he had composed a polka. At fourteen, with no formal training in composition, he wrote a concerto for flute and piano and a trio for two violins and 'cello.

Besides piano, Borodin studied the flute, and, in order to play string quartets, taught himself the 'cello. Quartet-playing soon became almost an obsession. To attend quartet sessions, Borodin would trudge seven miles with his 'cello under his arm. Once, it is recorded, the group played for twenty-four hours without stopping.

Borodin had another interest, chemistry. In his own room he set up a laboratory, where he conducted chemical experiments and made fireworks.

At seventeen he entered the Academy of Medicine

and Surgery, where he made a brilliant academic record. In May, 1858, he received his M.D. degree. He interned at the Second Military Hospital, where he met a bored young Guards officer named Mussorgsky, serving as Officer of the Day.

Borodin's real love, however, was research chemistry rather than medical practice. He went to Heidelberg to continue his scientific studies, remaining there from 1859 to 1861.

In Heidelberg he heard a great deal of music; had eight scientific papers published in Russian, French and Italian magazines; and met and became engaged to a pianist from Moscow, Catherine Protopopova, who had gone to Heidelberg for a "cure."

They were married on their return to St. Petersburg, where Borodin was appointed to the faculty of the Academy of Medicine. He was a well-liked teacher, not only for his brilliance but for his kindly manner toward his students. "When working in his laboratory," one of them recalled, "we felt as if we were in our own home."

At this time, through Mussorgsky, he came under the spell of Balakirev. "Until then," Balakirev recalled, "he had regarded himself as a mere amateur, and ascribed no importance to the impulse that drove him toward musical composition. I believe I was the first to tell him that composition was his real business. He eagerly started work on his Symphony in E-flat. Every bar of it was criticized and overhauled by me—which may have contributed to developing his critical sense, and finally determining his musical tastes and sympathies."

To be "criticized and overhauled" by Balakirev

could be trying. At one point he called for revisions in the Second Symphony, and, when Borodin had made them, for further revisions. This left the music exactly as Borodin had written it in the first place.

Fortunately, Borodin's temperament was easygoing, and Balakirevian whimsy left him unruffled. "If Borodin would only lose his temper!" Mussorgsky once exclaimed.

In the fall of 1865, Rimsky-Korsakoff met the Borodins and became a frequent visitor at their apartment. In the laboratory which adjoined it, Rimsky-Korsakoff would watch, fascinated, as the chemist distilled colorless gas from one retort to another, and would assure him he was "transferring emptiness into vacancy"—the Russian expression for "killing time."

In the midst of playing or talking about music, Borodin would suddenly rush to the laboratory to make sure nothing had boiled over—"filling the air, as he went, with incredible sequences of sevenths and ninths, bellowed at the top of his voice."

Borodin's working day, said Rimsky-Korsakoff, was "rather queerly arranged." Catherine Borodin suffered from insomnia and had to have a nap during the day, often sleeping until four or five in the afternoon. Sometimes they did not dine until eleven. Rimsky-Korsakoff often stayed until three in the morning and, to get home, had to cross the Neva in a rowboat, the wooden Liteyny drawbridge being opened for the night.

"Borodin," Rimsky-Korsakoff recalled, "was a man of strong physique; a man of no whims and easy to get along with. He slept little, but could sleep on anything and anywhere. He could dine twice a day, or go dinnerless altogether, both of which happened frequently."

Borodin needed self-possession; his home life was "one unending disorder. His inconvenient apartment, so like a corridor, never allowed him to pretend he was not at home to anybody. Dear old Borodin would get up with his meal or his drink half-tasted, would listen to all kinds of requests and complaints, and would promise to 'look into it.' People would gabble and chatter by the hour, while he himself constantly wore a hurried look, having this or that still to do.

"Catherine Sergeyevna continually passed sleepless nights. Alexander Porfiryvich had a difficult time with her at night, rose early, and got along with insufficient sleep. . . . Their apartment was often used as shelter by various poor relations who picked that place to fall ill or even lose their minds. Borodin had his hands full with them, doctored them, took them to hospitals and visited them there. In the four rooms of his apartment there often slept several strange persons of this sort; sofas and floors were turned into beds. Frequently it was impossible to play the piano because someone lay asleep in the adjoining room.

"At dinner, several tom-cats that found a home in Borodin's apartment paraded across the dinner-table, sticking their noses into plates, leaping unceremoniously to the diners' backs. These tom-cats basked in Catherine Sergeyevna's protection. One was in the habit of fetching homeless kittens by the neck to Borodin's apartment; these the Borodins would harbor, later finding homes for them.

"You might sit at their tea-table—and behold! Tommy marches along the board and makes for your plate. You shoo him off, but Catherine Sergeyevna takes his part and tells some incident from his biography. Meantime, zip! another cat has bounded at Alexander Porfíryvich and twined himself about his neck. 'Listen, dear sir, this is too much of a good thing!' says Borodin, but without stirring; and the cat lolls blissfully on."

Later, Rimsky-Korsakoff was to lose patience with his friend for spending so much time on "causes" as to leave none for chemistry or composition. Rarely was he to be found in his laboratory or at the piano. It usually turned out that he was just leaving for, or just returned from, a committee meeting; or that he had spent the day doing errands for one of the organizations to which he belonged because of constitutional inability to say "No."

"It always seemed odd to me," said Rimsky-Korsakoff "that certain ladies, who apparently were admirers of Borodin's talent as composer, mercilessly dragged him to all sorts of charitable committees, harnessed him to the office of treasurer, and so forth, and thereby robbed him of the time which could have been used for creating wonderful musical works. Thanks to the charitable hurly-burly, his time was frittered away on trifles that could have been attended to by such as were not Borodins."

One cause for Rimsky-Korsakoff's concern was that Borodin's great masterpiece, *Prince Igor*, had begun to take shape; but owing to the pressure of other activities, Borodin was making little progress with the opera. By every means in his power, Rimsky-Korsakoff tried to get "dear old Borodin" to hurry it along.

"One might come again and again and keep demanding how much he had written. Net results: a page or two of score, or else—nothing at all. To the query: 'Alexander Porfiryvich, have you been writing?,' he would reply, 'I have.' Then it would turn out that he had been writing a batch of letters. 'Alexander Porfiryvich, have you transposed that aria yet?' 'Yes, I have.' 'Well, thank the Lord! At last.' 'I transposed it from the piano to the table.'"

Meanwhile the Polovtsian Dances from *Prince Igor* and the closing chorus had been scheduled for a concert at the Free Music School. The voice parts were complete, and had been rehearsed by Rimsky-Korsakoff with the school chorus. But the orchestration was not completed; nor was there any assurance that it ever would be.

Rimsky-Korsakoff heaped abuse and reproaches on the unfortunate composer, and, finding this to have no effect, in desperation offered to help with the scoring himself:

Thereupon he came to my house in the evening, bringing with him the hardly-touched music of the Polovtsian Dances; and the three of us—Borodin, Liadov and I—took it apart and began to score it in hot haste. To save time we wrote in pencil rather than ink. Thus we sat at work until late at night. The finished sheets of the score Borodin covered with liquid gelatin to keep the pencil-marks intact. In order to have the sheets dry the sooner, he hung them out like wash on lines in my study. Thus the number was finished and passed on to the copyist.

Getting *Prince Igor* finished came to be almost an obsession with Rimsky-Korsakoff. Having some time free in the spring of 1885, he set to work at a "provisional piano score" of the opera, which at that time consisted of a few scenes complete and fully orchestrated, others in short-score or fragmentary sketches, and still others which existed only in the composer's mind.

"I imagine that Borodin will be captivated by my endeavors," Rimsky-Korsakoff wrote to the Moscow critic S. N. Kruglikov, "and will even do some of the work himself. In Act III his hand is needed. A great deal is still missing there. Oh, mighty *Koochka!*"

Borodin fussed and tinkered with *Prince Igor* for eighteen years—a long time, when it is recalled that *Rigoletto* was written in forty days, *The Messiah* in twenty. At his death he left it incomplete. The overture was written down by Glazounov from memories of hearing Borodin play it at the piano. (This feat was not quite so prodigious as it sounds, since all the themes of the overture occur elsewhere in the opera). Rimsky-Korsakoff, who from talks with Borodin was familiar with the over-all plan of the work, with Glazounov's assistance filled out Borodin's incomplete sketches and put the various numbers in order. *Prince Igor* has held the stage, after a fashion, ever since.

One reason for Borodin's delay in completing *Prince Igor* was his preoccupation with other works. He shelved the opera while writing his Symphony No. 2 in B Minor; laid it aside again to compose "In the Steppes of Central Asia," the work which first established his reputation outside Russia; and again for the String Quartet in A, which was coolly received in Russia but which, the composer proudly noted, had four performances in one season at Buffalo, New York.

Occasionally Borodin traveled abroad to see what the European chemists were up to. On one such trip he went to Weimar, where Liszt received him with great cordiality. To his wife Borodin wrote an amusing account of Liszt and his entourage; Weimar, he said, was "a Venusberg in which Liszt was Venus."

He also noted that Liszt told him: "Your Second Symphony is entirely new; nobody has done anything like it. And it is perfectly logical in structure."

On two successive trips to Belgium he was able to observe the success of his works, and to decline, with thanks, an invitation to conduct them.

Soon thereafter he began to compose a Third Symphony—putting *Igor* aside once more. On February 26, 1887, he wrote to his wife, who was ill in Moscow: "My beloved, I shall not be able to come to see you during Carnival week. I find I have to appear before a magistrate as a witness. Tomorrow we are having a dance. It will be '*grandement beau.*' I shall say no more about it and leave the description of the festivity to the more expert pen of your other correspondents."

The dance was one given by the academy professors. Borodin, who had been working at his Third Symphony all day, appeared in a Russian peasant costume. He was in high spirits and appeared to be enjoying himself immensely. In the midst of a conversation he collapsed from a heart attack and died on the spot.

IN THE STEPPES OF CENTRAL ASIA

Borodin wrote this "orchestral sketch" in 1880 to commemorate the twenty-fifth year of the reign of the Tsar Alexander II. It is dedicated to Liszt, who was fascinated by the work. When Borodin paid his second visit to Liszt at Weimar in 1881, the abbé begged him to make a four-piano arrangement before doing anything else.

It was this piece, more than any other, which first established Borodin's reputation as a composer. Borodin wrote to a friend in 1886 that "it has made the rounds of Europes, from Christiana to Monaco."

"In the Steppes" is a musical description of an Oriental caravan, escorted by Russian soldiers, crossing the sandy steppes. Russian and Oriental folk themes are combined with great ingenuity. The music dies away as the caravan passes out of sight.

Ansermet's fine, well-modulated treatment of the score shows this orchestral craftsman at his best. Fiedler's, too, is an excellent performance, and Stokowski's glows with hectic orchestral excitement.

Weldon's is a straightforward, untemperamental interpretation; those of Fournet and Fricsay are capably done; Mitropoulos' is somewhat erratic.

—Paris Conservatory Orchestra, Ernest Ansermet, cond. LONDON LL-864 (with Glinka: *"Russlan and*

Ludmilla" Overture; Mussorgsky: *A Night on Bald Mountain*; Prokofieff: *"Classical" Symphony*)

—Boston Pops Orchestra, Arthur Fiedler, cond. RCA VICTOR LM-2202 (with *"Prince Igor" Overture and Polovtsian Dances*; Rimsky-Korsakoff: *"Russian Easter" Overture*)

—Leopold Stokowski and his Symphony Orchestra. RCA VICTOR LM-1816 (with Mussorgsky: *A Night on Bald Mountain*; *Overture to "Khovantschina"*; Rimsky-Korsakoff: *"Russian Easter" Overture*)

—Hallé Orchestra, George Weldon, cond. MERCURY 50137 (with *"Prince Igor" Overture*; Rimsky-Korsakoff: *"Flight of the Bumblebee"*; Mussorgsky: *A Night on Bald Mountain*; Khachaturian: *"Gayne" Ballet Suite*)

—Lamoureux Orchestra, Jean Fournet, cond. EPIC LC-3432 (with Mussorgsky: *A Night on Bald Mountain*; Rimsky-Korsakoff: *Capriccio Espagnol*; Glinka: *Kamarinskaya*)

—Lamoureux Orchestra, Ferenc Fricsay, cond. DECCA 9859

—New York Philharmonic, Dimitri Mitropoulos, cond. COLUMBIA CL-751 (with *Polovtsian Dances*: Ippolitov-Ivanov: *Caucasian Sketches*)

NOCTURNE, FROM STRING QUARTET IN D

One of Borodin's most notable melodies—it has, like the Polovtsian Dances, even been turned into a popular song—this excerpt from the Quartet in D is a fine vehicle for showing off the string section of a first-rate orchestra. The Philadelphia Orchestra performance is beautifully done, with fine singing sound. The Stokowski version has the usual lush Stokowski tone and the usual Stokowski flourishes.

—Philadelphia Orchestra Strings, Eugene Ormandy, cond. COLUMBIA ML-5187 (with Tchaikovsky: *Serenade*; Barbar: *Adagio for Strings*; Vaughan Williams: *Fantasia on Greensleeves*)

—Leopold Stokowski and his Orchestra. CAPITOL PAO-8415 (with: *Music for Strings*)

POLOVTSIAN DANCES, FROM PRINCE IGOR

The much-recorded Polovtsian Dances, which in the opera take place during the festivities in honor of Igor and Prince Vladimir at the Polovtsian camp, offer listeners a wide choice of performers on disks. There is even a two-piano recording by Vronsky and Babin and an organ recording by Richard Ellsasser.

For that matter, one could get the original-cast recording of *Kismet*, a 1953 musical whose creators helped themselves to *Prince Igor* and other works so generously that a standing joke predicted Borodin would get the Drama Critics Circle Award that year.

Less amused was the French Society of Composers, Authors and Publishers, which sought to enjoin Producer Jack Hylton from taking *Kismet* to London in the spring of 1955. Unlike American copyrights, which last fifty-six years from the date of original copyrighting, European copyrights extend fifty years after the death of the author or authors. Rimsky-Korsakoff and Glazounov were virtually co-composers of *Prince Igor*, and Glazounov did not die until 1936. Hence the contention that the opera, assigned by Glazounov's heirs to a Parisian publisher, was still protected.

When asked for something in writing, the French replied that relevant documents were destroyed in the Reichstag fire.

That made the English judge laugh, says Hylton, although as a matter of fact the archives *were* in a building next to the Reichstag.

Kismet was produced in London anyway, and the French litigants, having lost in the lower courts, are planning an appeal to the House of Lords.

Among more conventional recordings, a place of honor, or perhaps the place of honor, should go to the performance by a chorus and orchestra led by Leopold Stokowski. Glowing, irridescent tone colors bring the music to vivid life.

Also sparkling is the performance by Markevitch and the Parisian forces. Dorati's is lively, but the sound engineering is uneven, marred by strident percussion and rough-voiced brass.

Among the spate of capable performances whose chief shortcoming is that there are so many others to choose from, might be mentioned Von Karajan's, Van Beinum's and Rodzinski's. And of great historic interest, as a memento of Stokowski's great days with the Philadelphia Orchestra, is the Camden re-issue, even though the sound is dated by today's hi-fi standards.

—Chorus and Symphony Orchestra, Leopold Stokowski, cond. RCA Victor lm-1054 (with De Falla: *El Amor Brujo*)
—Chorus and Radiodiffusion Française Orchestra, Igor Markevitch, cond. Angel 35144 (with Mussorgsky: A *Night on Bald Mountain*; Tchaikovsky: "*Romeo and Juliet*")

—Chorus and London Symphony Orchestra, Antal Dorati, cond. MERCURY 50122 (with Rimsky-Korsakoff: *"Coq d'Or" Suite*)

—Philharmonia Orchestra, Herbert von Karajan, cond. ANGEL 35307 (with: *Operatic Ballet Music*)

—London Philharmonic Orchestra, Eduard van Beinum, cond. LONDON LLP-203 (with De Falla: *El Amor Brujo*)

—London Philharmonic Symphony Orchestra, Artur Rodzinski, cond. WESTMINSTER XWN-18542 (with Mussorgsky: *A Night on Bald Mountain*; Ippolitov-Ivanov: *Caucasian Sketches*)

—Philadelphia Orchestra, Leopold Stokowski, cond. CAMDEN 203 (with Stravinsky: *"Petrouchka" Ballet Suite*)

—RIAS Symphony Orchestra, Ferenc Fricsay, cond. DECCA 9546 (with Dvořák: *Slavonic Dances*)

—Boston Pops Orchestra, Arthur Fiedler, cond. RCA VICTOR LM-2202 (with *"Prince Igor" Overture; In the Steppes;* Rimsky-Korsakoff: *"Russian Easter" Overture*)

—Bamberg Symphony Orchestra, Jonel Perlea, cond. VOX 9530 (with Mussorgsky: *A Night on Bald Mountain;* Balakirev: *Tamar;* Cui: *Tarantella*)

—New York Philharmonic, Dimitri Mitropoulos, cond. COLUMBIA CL-751 (with *In the Steppes;* Ippolitov-Ivanov: *Caucasian Sketches*)

—Los Angeles Philharmonic Orchestra, Alfred Wallenstein, cond. DECCA 9727 (with Ippolitov Ivanov: *Causcasian Sketches;* Enesco: *Rumanian Rhapsody No. 1*)

—Vronsky and Babin, duo-pianists. DECCA 9791 (with: *Dances*)

—Richard Elsasser, organist, MGM E-3127 (with: "*Concert Favorites*")

PRINCE IGOR

This wonderful opera is a score filled from end to end with music of enchanting beauty. Owing to the haphazard manner in which it was written, it is also rambling and discursive. In the first act, for example, Borodin vividly characterizes an interesting rascal, Prince Galitzky, an operatic first-cousin to Baron Ochs in *Der Rosenkavalier*. Galitzky then disappears from the opera. It is hypothesized that Borodin was planning to use him later but never got around to it.

The opera, moreover, is very long—so long that an uncut performance, even in Russia, is a rarity. The usual custom is to omit Act III entirely, which is done in the Period set. The London version is complete. Requiring five disks instead of three, it is, naturally, more expensive. The abridged version contains most of the opera's famous passages—the Overture, the Polovtsian Dances, Igor's aria and the love scene between Prince Vladimir and Princess Kontchakovna—and may therefore appeal to listeners as the better bargain of the two.

Both are excellent performances by fine casts of vocalists. As recorded sound, the London performance has a bit the best of it.

—Soloists, chorus and orchestra of the Belgrade National Opera, Oscar Danon, cond. Five 12-in. LONDON A-4503
—Soloists, chorus and USSR State Orchestra, A. Melik-Pashaev, cond. Three 12-in. PERIOD 552

Quartet No. 1 in A

In 1875, Borodin began planning a string quartet, "to the great distress of Stassov and Mussorgsky," he reported in a letter. Their distress was caused by the fact that he had given up work on *Prince Igor* to write the quartet. It was this work which, the composer proudly reported, had been done in Buffalo, New York.

The fluently-written quartet shows that its composer benefited from his practical experience as a quartet-player. It also shows his innate flair for contrapuntal writing. At twenty-two he was spontaneously writing fugues, a skill which others of the Five lacked and which Rimsky-Korsakoff had to acquire laboriously in mid-career.

The quartet receives sympathetic handling from the Konzerthaus players.

—Vienna Konzerthaus Quartet. WESTMINSTER XWN-18715

Quartet No. 2 in D

The Second String Quartet, dedicated to his wife, was not published until after Borodin's death. It is more lyrical and intimate in style than the Quartet No. 1. Its slow movement, arranged for string orchestra, is an orchestral favorite. (See note on "Nocturne.")

A sensitive, thoughtful performance is that by the Armenian State Quartet. Polish, refinement and elegance characterize the Galimir Quartet's playing. The Endres and Hollywood disks, while not quite up to the same level, are satisfactory.

—Armenian State String Quartet. ANGEL 35239 (with Shostakovitch: *Quartet No. 1*)

—Galimir Quartet. PERIOD 505 (with Glazounov: *Chanteurs de Noël*; Liadov: *Glorification*; Rimsky-Korsakoff: *Khorovod*)

—Endres Quartet. VOX 10190 (with Smetana: *Quartet No. 1*)

—Hollywood String Quartet. CAPITOL P-8187 (with Tchaikovsky: *Quartet in D*)

SYMPHONY NO. 1 IN E-FLAT

When Borodin, encouraged by Balakirev, decided to turn to composition, he did not do it by halves. No experimenting with smaller forms; Borodin plunged straightway into his Symphony in E-flat. "Every bar," said Balakirev, "was criticized and overhauled by me."

The work made slow progress, said Rimsky-Korsakoff, because of Borodin's inexperience at instrumentation—to say nothing of his somewhat hectic mode of life. Begun about 1862, it was finished in 1867 and had its first performance two years later. It was well received, and was one of the first works of the Five to become known outside Russia.

A minority disagreed, calling the work "freakish" and "amateurish." It is difficult even to guess whether these complaints were justified; Borodin revised the score completely in later years. As it now stands, much of it is typical of Borodin at his best, showing his rich gift of melodic invention and his sure sense of orchestral color.

The available recording by Galliera and the Philharmonia forces is excellent.

—Philharmonia Orchestra, Alceo Galliera, cond. ANGEL 35346 (with Rimsky-Korsakoff: *Capriccio Espagnol*)

SYMPHONY NO. 2 IN B MINOR

One reason for the delay in completing *Prince Igor* was the composer's habit of shelving the opera to work at other things. In 1870 he put it aside to begin his Second Symphony. The work utilized, among other things, a number of ideas conceived for *Prince Igor* which could not be fitted into the scheme of the opera.

The symphony had its first performance, in 1877, under difficult circumstances. In his hectic whirl of lectures, committee meetings, consultations and research, Borodin lost the manuscripts of the first and last movements. On top of this he had to go to bed with a high temperature. There were still a few days before the performance. The ailing doctor-composer sat in bed re-orchestrating, and exclaiming: "Never has a professor of the Academy of Medicine been found in such a position!"

The symphony was hastily and inadequately rehearsed; and in addition Borodin had been over-optimistic about the ability of the new chromatic brass instruments to execute rapid passages. Rescored, and adequately rehearsed, the B Minor Symphony has won for itself an enduring place in orchestral repertory.

Kletzki's reading of the work has great intensity;

his playing of the slow movement is the most expressive of the available performances. Ansermet's is on a smaller scale, marked by elegance and refinement rather than grandeur. The Dorati reading is powerful but erratic, with, seemingly, no over-all concept of the work to give the performance unity and coherence. The performances under Mitropoulos and Pflueger are adequate but not distinguished.

A further merit of the Ansermet recording is that it is rounded out with Borodin's unfinished Third Symphony in A Minor.

—Philharmonia Orchestra, Paul Kletzki, cond. ANGEL 35145 (with Ippolitov-Ivanov: *Caucasian Sketches*)

—Orchestre de la Suisse Romande, Ernest Ansermet, cond. LONDON LL-1178 (with *"Prince Igor"* Overture; *Symphony No. 3*)

—Minneapolis Symphony, Antal Dorati, cond. MERCURY MG-50004 (with Stravinsky: *"Firebird" Suite*)

—New York Philharmonic, Dimitri Mitropoulos, cond. COLUMBIA ML-4966 (with Tchaikovsky: *Suite No. 1*)

—Leipzig Philharmonic Orchestra, Gerhard Pflüger, cond. URANIA 7148 (with Tchaikovsky: *"1812" Overture; Capriccio Italien*)

CUI

Biographical Sketch

CÉSAR CUI, born in Vilna on January 18, 1835, was the son of a French officer who had remained in Poland after the Napoleonic campaign, had married a Lithuanian girl and had become a teacher of French at a Vilna school. Hence, unless his mother was of partly Russian descent (of which no evidence has turned up so far), Cui was a "Russian" composer only by virtue of residence in St. Petersburg.

Like others of the Five, Cui showed musical talent early. At fourteen he began composing mazurkas and nocturnes which he later described as "naïve imitations of Chopin." A friend thought them worth showing to Tadeusz Moniuszko, composer of *Halka* and other operas. Moniuszko was interested in young Cui's talent, and for seven months gave him lessons in harmony and counterpoint.

The lessons were cut short when Cui was sent to the School for Military Engineers in St. Petersburg. During the next four years he had little time for musical studies. It was only by becoming acquainted with Balakirev that he re-entered the world of music.

Balakirev was impressed by the fact that Cui had studied under a well-known composer. Rimsky-

Korsakoff has recorded that Balakirev and Cui were the "senior members" of the Five, at whose feet he, Borodin and Mussorgsky sat in respectful admiration.

Balakirev and Cui complemented each other to some extent; Balakirev had had no formal training in theory, as Cui had; but Cui was sadly deficient in instrumentation, and here Balakirev's wealth of practical knowledge and experience was valuable. Balakirev himself orchestrated the overture to Cui's first opera, *The Prisoner of the Caucasus,* and assisted with the scoring throughout.

In 1858 Cui married the singer Malvina Bamberg, and for her composed a light opera, *The Mandarin's Bride.* Three years later he began a more ambitious opera, based on Heine's tragedy, *William Ratcliffe.*

The composition of *William Ratcliffe* occupied Cui for the next seven years. His other duties left him scant time for composition. He had become an engineering officer, specializing in fortifications. In addition, he had opened a "cramming" school to prepare candidates for the School for Military Engineers, and was teaching most of the classes himself. And he was the music critic of an important newspaper, the St. Petersburg *Vyedomosti.*

As critic, Cui spared neither friend nor foe. He had constituted himself the spokesman for the Five, whom he somewhat bumptiously proclaimed the musical hope of Russia. But all the members of the *Koochka* got their lumps from Cui in the *Vyedomosti* at one time or another.

Cui sniped incessantly at Anton Rubinstein and the "Conservatory party," whose members tended to conservatism and whose musical orientation was strongly Germanic. He lost no opportunity to minimize Tchaikovsky.

As a result of these critical labors, when Cui's own *William Ratcliffe* was put up for performance it made a conspicuous target.

William Ratcliffe is perhaps not so bad as the reviews of 1869 made it appear to be. (A revival in 1900 was favorably received in Moscow.) At any rate, it was withdrawn after seven performances.

Undismayed, Cui wrote six more operas, and in 1881 revised his early *Prisoner of the Caucasus*.

During all this time, Cui's military career was flourishing. He had become a recognized authority on fortifications, and held professorships at the Artillery and Engineering schools. He wrote various technical manuals which in military circles were regarded as authoritative, and rose to the rank of Lieutenant General of Engineers.

In the later part of his life, Cui devoted himself to songs and brief instrumental works. These, as many critics have pointed out, show an almost total lack of originality, but are redeemed by their Schumannesque grace and charm.

Cui in his seventies remained youthful-looking and alert. In 1911 he wrote a parody of Debussy, which he called "*L'Après-midi d'un faune qui lit son journal.*" At the age of eighty he undertook the completion of Mussorgsky's unfinished *Sorochintsy Fair*, which, incredible as it seems in view of the political situation at that time, was performed in St. Petersburg in October, 1917. Cui died in March, 1918, at the ripe age of eighty-three.

TARANTELLA, OP. 12

Of the Five, Cui is most poorly represented on disks, only a single item being at present in the repertory. Perhaps some day an enterprising record company will bring out *William Ratcliffe* or *The Prisoner of the Caucasus*. Meanwhile, the orchestral Tarantella which Cui wrote in 1859 is heard in a jaunty performance by Perlea and the Bamberg forces.

—Bamberg Symphony Orchestra, Jonel Perlea, cond. Vox 9530 (with Balakirev: *Tamar;* Borodin: *Polovtsian Dances;* Mussorgsky: *A Night on Bald Mountain*)

MUSSORGSKY

Biographical Sketch

MODESTE PETROVICH MUSSORGSKY was born on March 21, 1839, on a big (forty square miles) estate near the village of Karevo in the province of Pskov. His father, Peter Mussorgsky, was the illegitimate son of a serf and an officer of the Preobrajensky Guards. Peter Mussorgsky's parents married after his birth; he was legitimized in 1820 and entered in the register of Pskov nobility. After a few years of government service in St. Petersburg, Peter Mussorgsky retired to his estate and married a lady who wrote poetry and bore him four sons, of whom the future composer was the youngest.

Little is known of Mussorgsky's early years except that he displayed precocious musical talent. At seven he was playing "short pieces" by Liszt, whose works, however, short, are difficult; at nine he played a concerto by John Field before a large audience in his father's house; at twelve he played at a charity concert.

At thirteen he entered the Cadet School of the Preobrajensky Guards.

By usual academic standards, the curriculum of the Cadet School was odd. Excessive study was felt to be beneath the dignity of an officer and a gentleman. Whenever he saw Mussorgsky bent over his desk, the general who headed the school would ask "*Mon cher*, what sort of officer will you make?"

The general objected to his cadets' drinking vodka like the common people, and reeling back to school on foot. But when a cadet was brought back in a carriage and pair, overcome by champagne, the general's delight knew no bounds.

It was little wonder that, after spending his formative years in this environment, Mussorgsky should have been author of the phrase, "To trans-cognac oneself."

In 1856 Mussorgsky left the Cadet School and entered the Preobrajensky Guards. That autumn he met Borodin, and through him, Balakirev. Borodin described the seventeen-year-old Mussorgsky as "a smallish, very elegant, dapper little officer; brand-new, close-fitting uniform; shapely feet; delicate, altogether aristocratic hands. Elegant, aristocratic manners; conversation the same, interspersed with French phrases, rather affected. Unusually polite and cultured. The ladies made a fuss over him. He sat at the piano and, coquettishly throwing up his hands, played excerpts from 'Trovatore,' 'Traviata,' etc., very pleasantly and gracefully, while the circle around him murmured in chorus, '*Charmant! Délicieux!*' "

Mussorgsky was soon studying composition with Balakirev. "Not being a theorist," Balakirev recalled later, "I could not—unfortunately—teach Mussorg-sky harmony, as Rimsky-Korsakoff teaches it now. But I used to explain the form of a composition to him. We played through all Beethoven's symphonies in four-hand arrangements, as well as many other compositions by Schubert, Schumann, Glinka and others. I explained to him the technical construction of the pieces we played, and he himself analyzed their form."

Mussorgsky had dabbled at composition during his student days. Among other things he had written a "Porte-Enseigne" Polka which his father had proudly had published, to the composer's later regret. Under the stimulus of the lessons with Balakirev he began composing again. But his work was hampered by a nervous disorder which attacked him at this time.

Resigning his commission in the Guards, Mussorgsky went with his brother Filaret to Tikhvin to take a "cure."

At about the same time Mussorgsky made his first visit to Moscow. It was one of the profoundest of his youthful experiences. The Kremlin fired his imagination, with results which were to be seen in *Boris Godunov*. At any moment, he wrote, he had half expected an ancient *boyar* to appear "in long smock and high cap."

Mussorgsky's debut as a composer was made January 23, 1860, when Anton Rubinstein conducted his Orchestral Scherzo in B-flat with considerable success. Next Mussorgsky toyed with the idea of writing an opera on the Oedipus legend and wrote a few choruses for it. Sketches for an opera based on Mengden's drama, *The Witch*, eventually became the orchestral work, "A Night on Bald Mountain." Mussorgsky began an Allegro in C for piano duet, and wrote the slow movement of a

Symphony in D, to be dedicated to the *Koochka*.

Meanwhile he was distracted by family problems. The Imperial order of March 3, 1861, for gradual emancipation of serfs over a two-year period brought serious financial hardship to most members of the landowning class in Russia. Peter Mussorgsky had died, and neither of his surviving sons displayed remarkable talent in practical affairs. Eventually Filaret, the elder brother, sold his father's estate and moved to a smaller one. Modeste returned to St. Petersburg, where he found a clerical job in the Ministry of Communications.

In October, 1863, Mussorgsky began sketching an opera based on Flaubert's *Salammbo*. The libretto which he put together was a patchwork, his own verses alternated with borrowings from Heine and Russian poets. Although the work was left unfinished, whole sections of it were later to be transferred to *Boris Godunov*.

He was also turning out a few songs, piano pieces and other works in smaller forms, and chafing over his musical dependence on Balakirev. In a letter to the older musician he charged him with "treating me as a child who has to be kept in leading-strings."

Others thought so too. "I believe if you withdrew your tutelage," Stassov wrote to Balakirev, "took him from the sphere where you have held him by force and set him free to follow his own devices and his own tastes, he would soon get overrun with weeds like all the rest. There's nothing inside him."

Balakirev's reply was terse and to the point; in

their estimates of one another, these Russian musicians did not mince words. "Mussorgsky," said he, "is almost an idiot."

The "idiot" meanwhile had lost his job in the Ministry of Communications—apparently because of a "reduction in staff" rather than any fault of his own, since he had recently had a promotion and three months later found another post in the Forestry Department.

He had also performed the curious experiment of setting to music a prose comedy, *The Marriage*, by Gogol. And he had conceived a bigger and bolder plan, that of making an opera out of Pushkin's youthful, quasi-Shakespearean drama, *Boris Godunov*.

The mere mention of *Boris Godunvo* generated enthusiasm. Mussorgsky conceived the idea in the early fall of 1868; in November the Russian Musical Society announced a program of "excerpts from the opera 'Boris Godunov,' by Mr. Mussorgsky." This was premature, since not a note had yet been put on paper; and the performance was postponed. But Mussorgsky had set to work with a will, and by the end of 1869 had turned out a full score of *Boris Godunov*.

"A" full score; not "the" full score. As will be shortly pointed out, no such thing as "the" full score of *Boris Godunov* exists.

Boris was submitted to the music committee of the Maryinsky Theatre, which consisted of four conductors, two violinists and a contrabass-player. It was rejected, six to one. Who dropped the single

white ball into the ballot-box has never been determined; every member of the committee is on
record with a disparaging comment of some sort
about *Boris*.

Mussorgsky then set to work revising *Boris*.
Among other things he added the entire "Polish
Act," the scene in Marina's dressing-room and the
love scene by the fountain. The composition of this
music "boiled," as Mussorgsky put it, on one occasion giving him no sleep for two nights running.

We think of the seductive Marina as so essential
a part of *Boris* that it is somewhat astonishing to
learn that she did not appear at all in the original
version. By the addition of the "Polish Act" Mussorgsky earned the gratitude of mezzo-sopranos for
all time to come. In the limited mezzo repertory,
Marina is a focal role hardly inferior to Carmen.

One such grateful mezzo was Y. F. Platonova, a
bright star of the Maryinsky Theatre. She wanted
to sing Marina. The Director of the theatre, Gedeonov, was cool to the idea. His was the standard
impresario's reaction: Why gamble on a new, ex-
perimental work when one could sell out with *Il
Trovatore?*

Telling the story long afterward, Platonova said
she refused to sign her 1873-74 contract until it was
stipulated that *Boris* would be performed. Skeptical
scholars looked up the contract and found no such
provision. It does seem clear, however, that Platonova's insistence was a chief factor in getting *Boris*
performed.

Gedeonov resubmitted the score to the music

committee. The committee again turned it down. Then Gedeonov himself made the decision to produce the opera.

Platonova said that next day Gedeonov summoned her, angry and excited, and shouted: "Well, My Lady, a pretty mess you've got me into. I run the risk of being expelled from the Service on account of you and your 'Boris.' And what good you see in it I can't make out—I've no sympathy whatever with your innovators, and now I've got to suffer for one of them!"

Boris was performed on January 27, 1874. Reviews were mixed, Cui's being especially hostile. In a letter to Stassov, Mussorgsky complained that "the tone of Cui's article is hateful. . . . And that attack on the composer's *self-satisfaction!* . . . Behind this insane attack, this deliberate lie I see nothing; it is as though objects were dimmed by the diffusion of soapy water through the air. *Self-satisfaction! Hasty composition! Immaturity!*"

Audience reaction, too, was mixed. Modeste Tchaikovsky reported both cheers and hisses when he heard *Boris* in its second season. His letter also records that it was a drastically pruned version of the score; the custom of making cuts in the voluminous opera evidently began early.

While *Boris* was obtaining a tenuous foothold in the repertory, Mussorgsky was already working on another opera, *Khovantschina*. Its composition went slowly. For one thing, Mussorgsky, again his own librettist, did not have his story clearly fixed in mind. For another, he was drinking heavily. He had come to lean more and more on Stassov for moral support, and now Stassov was in western Europe.

"It was really incredible," said the painter Repin, "how that well-bred Guards officer with his beautiful manners, that witty conversationalist with ladies, that inexhaustible punster, directly he was left without Stassov, quickly sank down, sold his furniture, even his elegant clothes, and took to haunting cheap restaurants where he settled down into the familiar type of 'has-been.' . . . How many times had Stassov, on his return from abroad, to dig him out of some cellar, nearly in rags, swollen with drink!"

Repin's well-known and extremely candid portrait depicts Mussorgsky with the confirmed toper's bleary eyes and red nose. (Mussorgsky used to say his nose had been frostbitten on parade during his Guards days.)

His friends were aware of Mussorgsky's situation, and concerned about it. Later Rimsky-Korsakoff was to write that "with the production of 'Boris' the gradual decadence of its highly gifted author has begun. Flashes of powerful creativeness continued for a long time, but his mental logic was growing dim, slowly and gradually."

In the midst of writing *Khovantschina*, Mussorgsky had conceived the idea of another opera, *Sorochintsy Fair*. Full of enthusiasm, he worked at the new opera for a time, then went back to *Khovantschina*, then worked simultaneously at both.

In 1878 Mussorgsky was transferred from the Forestry Department to the Inspection Commission of Government Control, which was headed by a music-lover named T. I. Filippov. Respecting Mussorgsky's genius, Filippov forgave Mussorgsky absolutely anything, though the latter did no work and very often arrived intoxicated after sleepless nights. Filippov never reprimanded him and, admitting this indulgent attitude, said, "I am the servant of artists!"

At the beginning of 1880, Mussorgsky was compelled to leave the Civil Service. Filippov and other friends came to his rescue, offering to supply him one hundred rubles a month, on condition that he finish *Khovantschina*. Ironically, another group of friends, unaware of this arrangement, offered him eighty rubles a month on condition that he finish *Sorochintsy Fair*. Mussorgsky accepted both offers, and, being compelled to work at both operas simultaneously, ended by finishing neither.

On February 23, 1881, Mussorgsky collapsed while accompanying a singer at a party, and was taken to the Nikolaevsky Military Hospital. "He is done for," Stassov informed Balakirev, "though the doctors say he may linger on for a year—or only a day."

It was at this time that Repin painted his unforgettable portrait of Mussorgsky, wearing Cui's dressing-gown. Cui and others of the *Koochka*, forgetting old animosities, gathered at the dying composer's bedside.

On March 27, a number of his friends came to visit Mussorgsky as usual. At five o'clock next morning, he cried out twice, and died.

Concerning the posthumous fate of Mussorgsky's operas, and of *Boris Godunov* in particular, there is in the folklore of music a legend which can be summarized approximately as follows:

"*Boris Godunov*, a bold, original work like nothing which had ever been heard before, was set upon by the pedantic Rimsky-Korsakoff with a view to preparing it for performance. Since mediocrity hates genius, Rimsky-Korsakoff toned down Mussorgsky's daring harmonies, gave his melodic line a more conventional turn, and sugar-coated his instrumentation. By this act of musical vandalism, Rimsky-Korsakoff debased a masterpiece into a cheap pot-boiler in the style of Italian opera. Let us therefore return to the true, original, unadulterated *Boris*."

A typical comment of this sort is Montagu-Nathan's: "A great deal of the so-called 'incorrect' or 'crude' is music that did not receive the sanction of his contemporaries, or of the immediately succeeding generation, for the simple reason that [Mussorgsky] was at least three generations ahead of his contemporaries. The advanced musician of the present day is, therefore, protesting against the emendations, because he finds in the original version something that he would himself be proud of having invented."

This statement is nonsense because there does not exist a manuscript which could be called a definitive "Original Version" of *Boris*. As already noted, Mussorgsky wrote two versions of the opera. The most nearly complete version is the composer's three-volume autograph full score, MS No. 37 in the Central Music Library of the State Theatres, Leningrad. This, however, omits the scene in Pimen's cell which explains who the False Dimitri is and what he is up to, and which must be picked up from a separate manuscript*—otherwise Dimitri's later appearance in the opera would be incomprehensible.

At various points the two versions duplicate, or, rather, contradict each other. Two manuscripts exist of the scene between Boris and his children. Both are in Mussorgsky's handwriting, both cover the same general situation in the opera, but the music and action are different. The second version contains a striking effect, Boris' nightmare with the musical clock. On the other hand, it contains the nurse's "Song of the Flea," the game with the whip and Feodor's story of the parrot, all irrelevancies which merely slow up the stage action.

Mussorgsky himself showed no clear-cut preference, which he could easily have done by destroying one version or the other. Which, then, is to be performed? The shorter first version? The second, despite its length? Which has greater musical merit? Somebody—editor or conductor—has to make the decision, which could hardly be described as "vandalism."

A great deal of confusion in regard to the "authentic" score of *Boris* originated in the following way:

In 1873, while negotiations were under way for the production of *Boris,* the St. Petersburg publisher Vassily Bessel undertook to bring out a reduction, for voices and piano, of the full score. Haste was essential; the vocal score had to be ready by the end of November, when the opera was to go into rehearsal.

Mussorgsky wrote a letter to Bessel dated May 14,

* When last heard from, among the "Rimsky-Korsakoff Papers" in the Russian Public Library, Leningrad.

in reply to "your letter of May 2," enclosing the
piano score: "Here it is—I've been as quick as I
could."

This was the vocal score of 1874, regarded by
most people until fairly recently as the "authentic"
version of the opera. The composer's full score was
not published until 1928. Comparison of the two
at once made clear that the vocal score of 1874 was
a hasty, inaccurate transcription of the full score.
Probably on account of time pressure, whole scenes
were omitted—that between the Overseer and the
people, for example, in Act I, and nine-tenths of
Pimen's narrative. Cuts were made in the Council
of Boyars scene, ending with the monologue and
death of Boris, mainly on account of the censor's
regulations.

There were also discrepancies in the music. The
orchestral phrase preceding the Overseer's appearance stands thus both in the Rimsky-Korsakoff edition and *in the composer's full score:*

In the vocal score of 1874 it appears as follows:

The concurrence of the full score and the version
made by Rimsky-Korsakoff (who, of course, worked
from the full score rather than the vocal score)
makes it seem possible that Version No. 2, above,
is a slip of the pen of the sort easily made by a
hurried and perhaps bleary-eyed copyist. It is also

the sort of error which engravers are likely to make, and which it is up to the composer to catch when he receives his "green proofs."

Proof-reading music, however, is a most exasperating job which requires time and quiet surroundings. Mussorgsky had little of either in the fall of 1873; the conductor Napravnik had announced that his other duties left him no time to rehearse *Boris*; consequently Mussorgsky himself was obliged to lead the rehearsals. In the midst of this furore, errors in the vocal score could have, and apparently did, slip by unnoticed.

But if one had learned *Boris* from the 1874 vocal score as the "authentic" version (and Mussorgsky's name, after all, was on the cover), one might justifiably have concluded from the Overseer's music and similar variants that Rimsky-Korsakoff had highhandedly tampered with the score for no apparent reason.

The 1874 vocal score caused no end of confusion. But it was in circulation, whereas the full score, when Rimsky-Korsakoff had finished with it, had gone to the Imperial library; and if the vocal score had errors and omissions it was not in Bessel's interest as a publisher to advertise that fact.

The hue and cry over "vandalism" reached full force in 1908, when Diaghilev produced *Boris* with sensational success in Paris. The fact is sometimes overlooked that *Boris* had been virtually forgotten in Russia until Rimsky-Korsakoff's revision appeared in 1896. The version Diaghilev used was Rimsky-Korsakoff's, which for some reason had been brought out not by Bessel, but by the rival firm of Belaiev. (Russian copyright arrangements, even today, are often incomprehensible to the Western mind.)

Bessel retaliated by distributing copies of the "authentic" 1874 vocal score among the Parisian music critics, who after comparing it with Rimsky-Korsakoff's jumped on the hapless reviser with both feet.

"Rimsky-Korsakoff's alterations," wrote Gaston Carraud, "are the most needless, incomprehensible and revolting thing of their kind ever done. Like an insect pest, he has gnawed away every characteristic detail in the work—everything that struck him as irregular because he was incapable of penetrating its logic."

And Jean Marnold declared: "No words could be harsh enough to pass adequate censure upon the shameful havoc wrought by Rimsky-Korsakoff. The clumsiness and ineptitude of his alterations suggest the mentality of a superannuated impresario or professional librettist."

Whether these strictures were deserved may be determined, now that the original full score is in print, by anyone willing to take the trouble to compare it with the Rimsky-Korsakoff version.

The final word in the controversy, however, will always be Rimsky-Korsakoff's: He had preserved and deposited in the Imperial library every scrap of manuscript pertaining to *Boris Godunov.* Anyone who did not like his arrangement of the opera was free to make a better one himself.

BORIS GODUNOV

Not having all the relevant facts at hand, French critics went to extremes in assailing Rimsky-Korsakoff for "vandalism" and charging him with pedantically correcting *Boris Godunov* as if it were a counterpoint exercise, thereby destroying its originality.

Their conclusions were reasonable since they did not know the 1874 piano score to be a hasty and incomplete transcription, and were unfamiliar with the Russian custom of leaving operas to be posthumously finished by Rimsky-Korsakoff.

Today the availability of the Russian State-Oxford University Press edition, based on the full score and with MS variants indicated in footnotes and appendices, makes it possible to assess Rimsky-Korsakoff's alterations in something like true perspective.

Robert Godet oversimplified matters in his *Les Deux Boris*. There are not two *Borises* but many. In Mussorgsky's handwriting there exists the music of the more or less complete full score, the piano score of 1874, which differs from it, and a bundle of autograph excerpts introducing further variants, and which, carelessly misnumbered by the critic V. V. Stassov, for a time created confusion as to the exact order of scenes. Obviously this hodge-podge must be put in order to be performable.

Just to make certain that confusion is complete, there are not one but two Rimsky-Korsakoff revisions. In 1908, stung by the needling of Diaghilev's Parisian customers, Rimsky-Korsakoff restored numbers omitted in his 1896 edition "because of the excessive length of the opera"—Pimen's narrative, the geography lesson, the scene of the parrot, the musical-clock episode, the scene between the false Dimitri and Rangoni, and Dimitri's monologue.

Assuming the full score to be the definitive and fully evolved form of *Boris Godunov,* it vindicates Rimsky-Korsakoff at point after point.

Where Rimsky-Korsakoff does deviate from the original, his changes are not always such as to "falsify" Mussorgsky. His rebarring of the 3/4 - 5/4 chorus in the opening scene into straight two-four time does not prove an objection to odd time-signatures as such. Rimsky-Korsakoff was fond of them himself (see note on *Sadko*) and in *Boris* left intact the alternating bars of 3/4 - 5/4 in Feodor's Act II aria. In any case, as a matter of practical performance the rebarring is not so drastic a change as it appears on paper.

In the second act, Xenia's aria is transposed up from D-flat to D and the nurse's "Song of the Flea" put down from G-flat to F. This may have been done to accommodate individual singers, or for orchestral reasons. All else being equal, in writing for orchestra composers avoid key-signatures with many sharps or flats, because these create difficulties for the transposing instruments. Half-tone transpositions like the two cited above make no essential change in the music and are an unadvertised feature of every season at the Metropolitan and other leading opera houses.

What about major alterations in the music? One such occurs in the Coronation Scene and is worth examining. The famous bell effect, beginning in eighth-notes, then eighths and sixteenths, and finally

sixteenth-notes, is an original and characteristic Mussorgskyan idea. Rimsky-Korsakoff, obviously thinking
it too good to waste, re-introduced it at the close of
the scene, where, besides adding a brilliant touch
of orchestral color, it helps to round out the design
of the piece into a satisfying A-B-A form with beginning, middle and end.

Is this "falsifying" Mussorgsky? It should be remembered that Rimsky-Korsakoff, as a result of
intimate friendship with the composer, knew not
only what he was able to get down on paper but
what he was trying to achieve. "How the bells used
to sound under Mussorgsky's fingers when he played
them at the piano!" Rimsky-Korsakoff recalled. In
the score it was another story, and Rimsky-Korsakoff accordingly took the matter in hand.

Rimsky-Korsakoff transposed the two final scenes,
feeling the opera ought to end with the death of
Boris. If one prefers to end with the strangely pro-
phetic scene in the forest near Kromy—the sky lit
by the fires of revolution as the Simpleton exclaims:
"Weep, Christian folk, for the enemy will come, and
blood will flow, and darkness will descend on Russia"—it is simplicity itself to reverse the order.

Poor old Rimsky-Korsakoff has got his lumps on
account of Boris, but in fairness it should be remembered that his arrangement rescued the forgotten opera from complete oblivion, even in Russia.
While the merits of this or that change could be
debated, the assertion that Rimsky-Korsakoff fell
upon a bold, daring, original work which he pretti-
fied and watered down to the level of an Italian
madrigal will not bear close examination.

And, when all is said and done, *Boris* as left by its composer is unplayable. When the Metropolitan staged its recent "original" version, it was necessary to engage the late Karol Rathaus to re-orchestrate the Coronation Scene and other weak spots, and pull the work together generally. The Rimsky-Korsakoff version, by contrast, is a neat package with all loose ends tied up, which can be put into rehearsal as soon as the score and parts arrive. For that reason it is chosen nine times out of ten, and is the version heard in these recorded performances.

One of the milestones of operatic recording is the sumptuous *Boris* recorded for His Master's Voice in Paris under the direction of Issay Dobrowen. The Bulgarian basso Boris Christoff, singing the title role, heads a notable cast which includes Eugenia Zareska, mezzo-soprano, Nicolai Gedda, tenor, Kim Borg, bass, and others.

The H.M.V. *Boris* at present is available on the RCA Victor label in this country. With the switch of allegiances between Electric and Musical Industries, Ltd., the parent organization of H.M.V., from Victor to Capitol, future issues will be released on the E.M.I.-Capitol label. (*Madama Butterfly* and *The Barber of Seville* have already made the transition.)

The Belgrade performance of *Boris*, though not quite so spectacular from an all-star cast standpoint, is a capably-sung, well-recorded performance, with the price advantage of being on three disks rather than four.

Both the Colosseum and Period sets appear to have been made from the same master, one of those "mystery tapes" which were frequently turning up from behind the Iron Curtain in the early days of LP.

—Eugenia Zareska, mezzo-soprano; Nicolai Gedda, tenor; Boris Christoff, bass; Choeurs Russes de Paris; Orchestre National de la Radiodiffusion Française, Issay Dobrowen, cond. Four 12-in. RCA VICTOR LM-6403
—Soloists, chorus and orchestra of Belgrade National Opera, Kreshmir Baranovich, cond. Three 12-in. LONDON A-4317
—Soloists, chorus and orchestra of the Bolshoi Theatre, N. Golovanov, cond. Three 12-in. COLOSSEUM CRLP-124/6
—Soloists, chorus and orchestra of the Bolshoi Theatre, Alexander Gauk, cond. Three 12-in. PERIOD 554

BORIS GODUNOV EXCERPTS
—Fedor Chaliapin (bass), chorus, orchestra. ANGEL COLH-100
—Boris Christoff (bass), *as above*. RCA-VICTOR LVT-1021

KHOVANTSCHINA

Left unfinished by Mussorgsky at his death, this opera was completed by Rimsky-Korsakoff partly from memory and partly from the composer's notes. There were the usual cries of "vandalism" and further tinkering was done by Ravel and Stravinsky.

Metropolitan Opera subscribers had their first sight of *Khovantschina* February 16, 1950, with Emil

Cooper conducting, Lawrence Tibbett as Prince Khovansky and Risë Stevens, Robert Weede and Jerome Hines in other principal roles.

Those who saw the Metropolitan production will remember the curiously mixed effect which the work produced. The "Scene by the River Moskva," with dawn breaking and the bells sounding for Matins, was a passage which, some listeners thought, made the "1812" Overture seem tame.

On the other hand, the work was handicapped by what the late Olin Downes called its "wonderful, awful, scrambled, semi-incomprehensible libretto" and the complete impossibility of realizing Mussorgsky's conception in actual theatre performance.

Mr. Downes put it aptly in describing *Khovantschina* as the torso of what might have been a masterpiece. As such it is given a sympathetic performance by the Belgrade forces.

—Sofiya Jankovich, soprano; Drago Startz, tenor; Miro Cangalovich, bass; Belgrade National Opera Chorus and Orchestra, Kreshmir Baranovich, cond. Four 12-in. LONDON A-4405

THE MARRIAGE

In 1868 Mussorgsky made an experiment which he called "opera dialogue." He attempted to set to music, exactly as it stood, Gogol's comedy, *The Marriage*.

How far this is at variance with usual operatic practice can be seen by comparing Verdi's *Rigoletto* with Hugo's *Le Roi s'amuse*, Puccini's *La Bohême* with Murger's *Scènes de la Vie de Bohème*, or

Puccini's *Tosca* with Sardou's. Spoken drama must undergo a tremendous amount of telescoping and condensing to make a usable libretto, since a sung text moves at a slower pace than dialogue.

In any case, Mussorgsky became bored with the project after completing one act. Ippolitov-Ivanov wrote music in Mussorgskyan style for the rest of the opera, which had its first complete performance in Moscow in 1931. Its importance is chiefly that of a historical curiosity which it is good to have on records, since in this country, at least, one will probably never encounter it in the opera house.

Westminster's vocalists do their best with the decidedly unoperatic material at their disposal.

—Alexandra Yakovenko, soprano; Pavel Pontriagin, tenor; Daniel Demyanov, baritone; USSR State Radio Orchestra and Chorus, Alexei Kovalev, cond. Two 12-in. WESTMINSTER OPW-1202

A NIGHT ON BALD MOUNTAIN

This work had a curious history. Mussorgsky had long been fascinated by the witches' Sabbat which tradition associated with the "Bald Mountain," Mount Triglav, near Kiev. The Black God, Tchernobog, presided in the shape of a goat over the Black Mass and witches' revel held on St. John's Eve, June 24.

Mussorgsky's first attempt to depict the scene in music took the form of a piece for piano and orchestra, influenced, according to Rimsky-Korsak-off, by Liszt's "Todentanz." We are obliged to take his word for it, since the score has disappeared.

Mussorgsky next utilized the "Bald Mountain" music in *Sorochintsy Fair*. It was a pure interpolation having little to do with the rest of the opera (see note on *Sorochintsy Fair*) and stuck out like a sore thumb. On the other hand, it was striking, characteristic Mussorgskyana of power and originality.

Rimsky-Korsakoff tells how for two years he mulled over the problem of utilizing the "Bald Mountain" music most effectively. Finally he threw out Mussorgsky's choral passages entirely, tightened and condensed the music and rescored it into an orchestral display-piece of spectacular brilliance. This time no one raised the cry of "vandalism"; the incandescent tone colors of "Bald Mountain," Rimsky-Korsakoff version, left criticism miles behind.

An especially exciting performance of the lively work is that by the Philharmonia under Giulini. Ansermet's is a musicianly, superbly controlled reading, though on a somewhat smaller and less flamboyant scale. The performance by Golovanov and the Soviet State Radio Orchestra, though less satisfying as recorded orchestral sound, offers an interesting Russian point of view on how the work ought to go—namely, pretty much as everyone else does it.

The Stokowski version is an interesting curiosity, made from the four-channel sound track of the Disney film, *Fantasia*. In its day it made recording history and still remains a walloping performance, but by present standards it is not high-fidelity and, says the album-liner, "no such claim is made."

The Rodzinski performance, while temperate, shows thorough comprehension of the music and complete mastery of the orchestra. Fournet's, Markevitch's and Perlea's are conventional, acceptable performances.

—Philharmonia Orchestra, Carlo Maria Giulini, cond. ANGEL 35463 (with Tchaikovsky: *Second Symphony*)

—Paris Conservatory Orchestra, Ernest Ansermet, cond. LONDON LL-864 (with Borodin: *In the Steppes*; Glinka: *"Russlan and Ludmilla"* Overture; Prokofieff: *"Classical"* *Symphony*)

—USSR State Radio Orchestra, Nikolai Golovanov, cond. VANGUARD 6000 (with Rimsky-Korsakoff, *"Coq d'Or"* Suite)

—Philadelphia Orchestra, Leopold Stokowski, cond. DISNEYLAND WDX-101 (with Bach: *Toccata and Fugue in D Minor*; Ponchielli: *Dance of the Hours*; Stravinsky: *Rite of Spring*)

—London Philharmonic, Artur Rodzinski, cond. WESTMINSTER XWN-18542 (with Borodin: *Polovtsian Dances*; Ippolitov-Ivanov: *Caucasian Sketches*)

—Lamoureux Orchestra, Jean Fournet, cond. EPIC LC-3432 (with Borodin: *In the Steppes*; Glinka: *Kamarinskaya*; Rimsky-Korsakoff: *Capriccio Espagnol*)

—Orchestre Nationale Française, Igor Markevitch, cond. ANGEL 35144 (with Tchaikovsky: *"Romeo and Juliet"*; Borodin: *Polovtsian Dances*)

—Bamberg Symphony, Jonel Perlea, cond. Vox 9530 (with Balakirev: *Tamar*; Borodin: *Polovtsian Dances*; Cui: *Tarantella*)

PICTURES AT AN EXHIBITION

In 1873, Victor Hartmann, painter, architect and close friend of Mussorgsky, died at the age of thirty-nine. Shortly after his death a memorial exhibition of Hartmann's works was arranged at the Academy of Arts in St. Petersburg. Mussorgsky, upon visiting the exhibition, resolved to set ten of the Hartmann pictures to music as a tribute to his dead friend.

Mussorgsky's original composition was for piano. Maurice Ravel, seeing its possibilities for orchestral display, made a transcription which became, and remains, a favorite of concert audiences.

So rich and varied is the LP catalogue that collectors have a choice of several fine recorded performances, both in Mussorgsky's original piano version and the Ravel transcription.

The piano version is superbly played by Vladimir Horowitz. "Pictures at an Exhibition" has long been a showpiece favored by this gifted pianist, and he performs it on the record with stupendous *brio*.

Hardly inferior is the recorded performance by Leonard Pennario, playing at the very top of his form. This record is one of Pennario's best.

The performances by Reisenberg, Malinin and Katchen are approximately on a par. All three are sound technicians who play the music with comprehension, if not quite matching the pyrotechnics of Horowitz and Pennario.

The much-recorded orchestral version offers a number of fine performances from which to make a selection. For sheer magnificence of recorded sound, the most dazzling record is that which won a Grand Prix du Disque for Antal Dorati and the Amsterdam Concertgebouw. Musical values are highlighted in the Toscanini-NBC Symphony performance. "Pictures at an Exhibition" was a Toscanini favorite, and the disk has the usual virtues of recordings approved by the finicky Maestro— great power and energy, loving attention to detail, stupenduous crescendos. Soundwise, this is one of the later—and better—NBC Symphony recordings.

If one finds the Toscanini performance too incisive and overdriven, as some listeners do, the Ansermet reading is an alternative of great distinction. Von Karajan's, too, is a sound, never-overdone performance close to the Ansermet standard.

Markevitch's well-recorded disk shows that the conductor has a keen ear for orchestral textures, but the performance is somewhat diffuse and lacks the grandeur of other available recordings.

Kubelik's interpretation has solid musical substance, and Ormandy's is notable as brilliant recorded sound. The Reiner performance is that of a seasoned veteran who keeps musical matters firmly in hand.

The late Guido Cantelli, whose promising career was prematurely ended by a plane crash, was not at his best in "Pictures at an Exhibition." Abendroth's version, while competently done, suffers from comparison with the best of the available performances.

ORIGINAL PIANO VERSION

—Vladimir Horowitz, pianist. RCA VICTOR LVT-1023

—Leonard Pennario, pianist. CAPITOL P-8323 (with Tchaikovsky: *Humoresque, Dumka, Romance in F Minor*)

—Nadia Reisenberg, pianist. WESTMINSTER XWN-18721

—Eugene Malinin, pianist. ANGEL 35317

RAVEL TRANSCRIPTION

—Amsterdam Concertgebouw Orchestra, Antal Dorati, cond. EPIC 3LC-3015 (with Dvořák: *Slavonic Rhapsody*; Smetana: *Die Moldau*)

—NBC Symphony Orchestra, Arturo Toscanini, cond. RCA VICTOR LM-1838 (with Franck: *Psyché*)

—Orchestre de la Suisse Romande, Ernest Ansermet, cond. LONDON LL-956 (with Ravel: *La Valse*)

—Philharmonia Orchestra, Herbert von Karajan, cond. ANGEL 35430

—Berlin Philharmonic Orchestra, Igor Markevitch, cond. DECCA 9782 (with Wagner: *Siegfried Idyll*)

—Chicago Symphony Orchestra, Rafael Kubelik, cond. MERCURY 50000

—Philadelphia Orchestra, Eugene Ormandy, cond. COLUMBIA ML-4700 (with Stravinsky: *"Firebird" Suite*)

—Chicago Symphony Orchestra, Fritz Reiner, cond. RCA VICTOR LM-2201

—NBC Symphony Orchestra, Guido Cantelli, cond.

RCA Victor lm-1719 (with Tchaikovsky: "*Romeo and Juliet*")

—Leipzig Philharmonic Orchestra, Hermann Abendroth, cond. Urania 7157 (with Stravinsky: "*Firebird*" Suite)

SONGS

MUSSORGSKY was unique among the Five in achieving distinction as a composer of songs. The form was obviously one in which he felt at home, writing fluently and idiomatically for voice and piano. Even Tchaikovsky, a prolific writer of vocal music, achieved nothing so fine as the cycles "Sunless," "The Nursery" and "Songs and Dances of Death." These show Mussorgsky at his most original and most characteristic, unhampered by the limitations of technique which made composing in larger forms and for more complex instrumentation a laborious trial-and-error process.

A labor of love on the part of Angel Records is its four-disk issue of the Mussorgsky songs, complete, as recorded by the fine basso Boris Christoff. The handsome package also includes an eighty-four-page book of musico-historic notes in Russian, English, French and Italian.

Some listeners may not go all the way with Angel's commentator, Guido Pannain, that the complete songs of Mussorgsky constitute a "music-drama" in themselves, a cycle connected by a "secret and invisible thread." But there can hardly be any question that they demonstrate the range and diversity of Mussorgsky's musical thought. "Little Star, Where Art Thou?", written when the composer was eighteen, is an odd, poignant song, with unexpected twists and turns of the vocal line resulting from use of the Phrygian mode common in Russian folk music. Other moods encountered range from the biting irony of "The Seminarian" through the dance-rhythm of "Hopak," the buffoonery of "Song of the Flea" and the tragic grandeur of "Death the Commander."

To all these varied moods Mr. Christoff brings the needed versatility and the zeal of a partisan. It was Mussorgsky's vocal music, he informs us in a prefatory note, which caused him to give up a law career in favor of singing. His realization of Mussorgsky's songs is a distinguished addition to the record repertory.

The soprano Maria Kurenko is in good voice for "The Nursery" cycle, and offers knowing, sympathetic interpretations of its contents.

Both Mr. Christoff and Miss Kurenko sing in Russian, the ideal choice for songs composed in that language. A translation, as everyone knows who has dabbled in translating, is an uneasy compromise between fidelity to the literal meaning of the original text, the preservation of the rhyme-scheme, and the demands of the musical line.

Irmgard Seefried accordingly is handicapped by the fact of performing the songs in German. Nevertheless, the fine musicianship and vocal distinction displayed by the soprano make her recording of "The Nursery" worth the attention of Mussorgsky collectors.

Heinz Rehfuss, despite his name, is a French-speaking Swiss who sings the "Songs and Dances of Death" in his mother tongue. His performance, although not vocally distinguished, is a sensitive, thoughtful recording of the cycle.

—Boris Christoff, bass; Orchestre Nationale de la Radiodiffusion Française, Georges Tzipine, cond.; Alexandre Labinsky, pianist. Four 12-in. ANGEL 35602/5

—Maria Kurenko, soprano; Vsevolod Pastukhoff, pianist. CAPITOL P-8265 (with Rachmaninoff: *Songs*)

—Irmgard Seefried, soprano; Erik Werba, pianist. DECCA DL-9809 (with Bartók: *Songs*; Brahms: *Songs*; Wolf: *Songs*)

—Heinz Rehfuss, baritone; Hans Willi Haeusslein, pianist. LONDON LL-1318 (with Wolf: *Songs*)

SOROCHINTSY FAIR

This opera was finished in circumstances which were complex, even for a Mussorgsky opera. Since it was left in fragments by the composer at his death, Anatole Liadov, at Rimsky-Korsakoff's suggestion, undertook to complete the work.

After doing five excerpts, Liadov lost interest. But in the meantime, Cui decided to have a go at the opera. He completed all the missing links and orchestrated the work in its entirety. *Sorochintsy Fair* had its first complete performance in St. Petersburg in October, 1917.

Next Tcherepnin made an arrangement of the opera, making use of all the material previously contributed by Liadov and Cui, and in addition borrowing music from *Boris Godunov* and other Mussorgsky works.

The latest revision is by the composer W. J. Shebalin, prepared from Mussorgsky's manuscripts in collaboration with the Mussorgsky scholar Paul Lamm, and with missing sections completed by Shebalin.

In whatever edition, *Sorochintsy Fair* is a patchwork. Its most famous passage, the Witches' Sabbat on Bald Mountain, is a pure interpolation having little relation to the rest of the story. It is seen in a dream by the young peasant Gritzko, who then wakes, and that is the end of the witches.

A fascinating comparison, however, is of "A Night on Bald Mountain" as heard here in its original form with the orchestral version evolved by Rimsky-Korsakoff.

Sorochintsy Fair is heard in an admirable performance by the Slovenian National Opera.

—Soloists, chorus and orchestra of the Slovenian National Opera, Samo Hubad, cond. Two 12-in. EPIC SC-6017

RIMSKY-KORSAKOFF

Biographical Sketch

THERE IS a curious similarity in the early days of the Five. All were brought up in well-to-do households where making music was a part of family life. In the case of Nicolai Rimsky-Korsakoff, it was the home of his father, Andrei, a retired provincial governor, at Tikhvin, where the future composer was born on March 18, 1844.

Young Nicolai's arrival may have been a surprise; his father was sixty, his mother forty-two, and the only other child in the family was twenty-two-year-old Voin.

Rimsky-Korsakoff's family were musical. His mother had once been a fluent pianist. His father played by ear melodies from the operas of Méhul, Rossini, Spontini and Mozart. At three, young Nicolai was expert at beating a drum in time to his father's piano-playing. At six he had his first piano lessons. He recalled that he had been an indifferent pupil; he played inaccurately and was weak at counting.

The Rimsky-Korsakoffs were "Navy people." Uncle Nicolai was an admiral; brother Voin was in the service and eventually would be an admiral also. Voin's letters home from a five-year cruise in the Far East fired young Nicolai's imagination. He eagerly read books about the sea, which he had not yet laid eyes on, and constructed model ships. At twelve he was taken by his father to St. Petersburg to enter the Corps of Naval Cadets.

In St. Petersburg there was available better piano-teaching than he had had at Tikhvin. There were other musical experiences, too, which came as a revelation. Music in Tikhvin had been limited to the family piano, and to the singing of the monks in the monastery across the river. In St. Petersburg the young cadet discovered the enchanted world of opera, through a performance of *Lucia di Lammermoor*. He also heard his first symphony concert, at which Glinka's "Jota Aragonese," he recalled, "simply dazzled me."

There were two summer cruises aboard the gunnery-training ship *Prokhor*, commanded by Voin Rimsky-Korsakoff. In June, 1858, Nicolai gave his brother a fright by falling from the mizzentop, fortunately landing in the sea rather than on deck. He was hauled out and escaped with bruises and a reprimand.

Nicolai lived in his brother's cabin, away from the other cadets. The brothers were devoted to each other, although due to the difference in their ages, Voin's attitude was almost paternal. There exists a charming letter to their parents in which Voin tells how he used one of Nicolai's youthful romances as a means of getting the boy to smarten up his appearance and perfect his French.

Nicolai enjoyed sailing, and mathematics, especially in its application to celestial navigation, was his best subject. He was fearless in going aloft. He was a strong swimmer, often circling the ship five times without stopping. He was never seasick and was never afraid of the sea and its perils.

But at bottom he did not like sea service and realized he had no aptitude for it. He had, according to his own estimate, "no executive ability and no presence of mind." He was unable to master the "voice of command."

Those were the days of fists and rope's-ends. A man earned distinction in the Russian Navy by his fluency and inventiveness in swearing, or by his skill in knocking out teeth when the drunken crew were brought aboard from shore leave. On several occasions young Nicolai witnessed the punishment of sailors with two to three hundred lashes on the bare back.

Ashore, he was bored by the "military humdrum" of the school. "In this atmosphere I vegetated, languid and emaciated."

It may be imagined that the seventeen-year-old cadet found Balakirev's bracing personality as refreshing as a sea breeze. Balakirev looked over the sketches which Rimsky-Korsakoff had amused himself by writing, pronounced them the work of a genius and set young Nicolai to work at writing a symphony.

In later years, when he had broken with Balakirev, Rimsky-Korsakoff looked back on this first assignment as a mistake. "Having made me write a symphony, he cut me off from preparatory work and the acquisition of a technique. . . . A truly talented pupil needs so little. It is so easy to show all that is necessary in harmony and counterpoint if only the thing is properly undertaken. A year or two of systematic study, a few exercises in free composition and orchestration, and the teaching is over, provided one has a good piano technique. The pupil is no longer a schoolboy, but a budding composer striking out for himself."

What Balakirev should have done, said Rimsky-Korsakoff, was to have given him lessons in harmony and counterpoint, and explained to him the grammar of musical forms. Balakirev of course, could not do so, since he did not possess this knowledge himself.

At all events the young composer plunged into his symphony, orchestrating it with the aid of Berlioz' treatise on instrumentation, and writing many passages which he later found to be unplayable. The work was finished, "in one way or another," in May, 1862.

In September Rimsky-Korsakoff's musical studies were interrupted by orders to sail as one of four midshipmen aboard the clipper *Almaz*. This was one of the Russian squadron whose arrival in New York Harbor was a significant event of the Civil War. Great Britain's sympathies were openly with the Southern cotton-planters who supplied the looms of Lancashire. In Mexico a French expeditionary force had landed; it was not withdrawn until President Johnson massed battle-seasoned troops on the Texas border in 1865. A joint Franco-British-Confederate push appeared a lively possibility. But Union negotiators had been busy, too, and in July,

1863, after a lengthy stopover in England for refitting, the Russian squadron put to sea with instructions to take its orders from Abraham Lincoln, and to prepare for war with any Power.

The squadron remained in U. S. waters from October, 1863 to April, 1864. In New York, Rimsky-Korsakoff heard "rather poor" performances of *Faust* and Meyerbeer's *Robert le Diable*, and played harmonium-and-violin duets with an American pilot named Thompson. Officers and midshipmen traveled via the Albany night boat to Niagara Falls, of which Rimsky-Korsakoff retained a vivid memory thirty years later. There were also visits to Annapolis, Baltimore and Washington.

In April, 1864, the clipper was ordered to Russia by way of Cape Horn and the Pacific. The *Almaz* put in at Rio de Janeiro, which enchanted Rimsky-Korsakoff; it put in again for repairs after springing a leak off Cape Horn. In April, 1865, it dropped anchor at Kronstadt, and Rimsky-Korsakoff's days as a seagoing naval officer were over.

Rimsky-Korsakoff was welcomed by the *Koochka*, now enlarged by the addition of Borodin. The *Almaz* had been dismantled and Rimsky-Korsakoff's shore duties were light—two or three hours' clerical work each morning. At Balakirev's prompting he overhauled his symphony, which Balakirev then conducted at a Free Music School concert. The performance was successful; Rimsky-Korsakoff surprised the audience by appearing in his naval uniform to take a bow. A month later it was repeated at a Theatre Concert under Constantine Liadov. Cui hailed Rimsky-Korsakoff in a *Vyedomosti* article as "the first to compose a Russian symphony."

Rimsky-Korsakoff kept working at other compositions, including the "Overture on Three Russian Themes," the "Serbian Fantasy," and quadrilles on themes from *Martha* and *La Belle Hélène* which he played for Sunday dancing at his brother's house— and kept a dark secret from Balakirev.

He was struggling to improve his piano technique, practicing scales in thirds and octaves and going through Czerny's *Daily Exercises*. He was groping, too, for a better way of solving composition problems than that of trial and error.

He had begun to suspect that Balakirev was not an altogether trustworthy guide. He was at work on a second symphony, but was not satisfied with it; nor were others of the *Koochka*. Balakirev's comment was that the symphony had "sauce and cayenne pepper, but no roast beef." This left Rimsky-Korsakoff as baffled as before; he put the symphony aside.

The ignorance of the *Koochka* in many important areas was in fact astonishing. Balakirev, despite his great experience as a conductor, does not seem to have realized that "natural-scale" brass had been replaced by valve-horns everywhere. Unaware of this, the *Koochka* blindly followed the obsolete rules of Berlioz' *Treatise*.

"We selected French horns in all possible keys in order to avoid the imaginary stopped notes," said Rimsky-Korsakoff. "We calculated, contrived and grew unimaginably confused. And yet all that would have been necessary was a talk and consultation with some practical musician."

By trial and error, however, Rimsky-Korsakoff's work continued. He was now sharing an apartment with Mussorgsky, who was as deep in *Boris Godunov* as he in *The Fair Maid of Pskov*. It was a congenial arrangement which increased the already existing friendship between the two composers. When Rimsky-Korsakoff was married, on July 12, 1872, to the pianist Nadejda Purgold, Mussorgsky was best man.

An event which was to have a profound influence on Rimsky-Korsakoff's career was the invitation to succeed Zaremba as Professor of Composition and Instrumentation at the conservatory. His hours would be so arranged that it would not be necessary to resign his Navy commission. Rimsky-Korsakoff accepted. Years later he recalled how ill-equipped he had been:

"Had I ever studied at all, had I possessed a fraction more of knowledge, it would have been obvious to me that I could not accept the appointment, that it was foolish and dishonest of me to become a professor. But I was young and self-confident, my self-confidence was encouraged by others, and I joined the Conservatory.

"And yet at the time I could not decently harmonize a chorale; I had hardly any notion of counterpoint or the structure of a fugue; I did not even know the names of chords.

"Perhaps it will be said that all the above information was unnecessary to the composer of 'Sadko' and 'Antar.' Of course, to compose an 'Antar' or a 'Sadko' is more interesting than to harmonize a Protestant chorale or write four-part counterpoint. But it is shameful not to know such things and to learn of their existence from one's own pupils."

But, having undertaken to teach at the conservatory, Rimsky-Korsakoff became one of its most diligent students. "I was aided by the fact that at first none of my pupils could imagine that I knew nothing; and by the time they had learned enough to see through me, I had learned something myself."

He hurled himself into the study of harmony and counterpoint, sitting down "so poorly informed that I found myself acquiring systematic knowledge even in elementary theory." The first fruit of these studies was a string quartet, featuring a double canon in *stretto* and other learned devices. Even Rimsky-Korsakoff at length was obliged to concede that it was not a very good quartet. "And this was because the technique had not yet entered my flesh and blood, and it was still too early for me to write counterpoint without imagining myself Bach or someone else."

Now the Navy had a surprise in store for him. The death of Admiral Voin Rimsky-Korsakoff ended a long-standing feud with N. K. Krabbe, Minister of Marine. But when his old antagonist was dead, Krabbe saw to it that the Admiral's mother, widow and children were well provided for, and informed his younger brother that he had been appointed Imperial Inspector of Naval Bands. It was a new post, created especially for Rimsky-Korsakoff. He was to visit all Navy bands throughout Russia and see to it that they were musically up to the mark. The work was not burdensome enough to interfere with his teaching or composing; the salary left him "rather well fixed" financially.

Rimsky-Korsakoff's first official act was to go to the country with a trunkful of woodwind and brass instruments and set out to learn to play them. Although, by his own admission, he acquired no virtuosity on any band instrument, he did master their basic principles, learning what any instrument could and could not be expected to do. He soon understood the difference between writing a passage of virtuoso difficulty and a passage which was unplayable. "I had learned what every practical musician knows, but what, unfortunately, artist-composers do not know at all." Balakirev's "mastery" of instrumentation, he now saw clearly, had been nine-tenths pure bluff.

Balakirev had gone into retreat at the Warsaw Railroad freight station. Although he had not resigned his directorship of the Free School, he never came near it and the concerts, on which the school depended for part of its income, languished. Rimsky-Korsakoff took over, programing works compatible with the contrapuntal frame of mind in which he found himself—Bach's B Minor Mass and *St. Matthew Passion*, Allegri's "Miserere," a Kyrie by Palestrina and excerpts from Handel's *Israel in Egypt*. Box-office receipts, according to Rimsky-Korsakoff, were splendid.

In 1878, Rimsky-Korsakoff began working at an opera based on Gogol's *May Night*. It was an important milestone in his artistic evolution; in this work, he said, he "cast off the shackles of counterpoint." Although contrapuntal devices abound in the score, they are employed easily, unself-consciously and solely for their appropriateness to the musical business at hand. Rimsky-Korsakoff, always analytical, found the recitatives somewhat awkward, and resolved to do better next time.

"Next time" was an opera based on Ostrovsky's drama, *The Snow-Maiden.* Rimsky-Korsakoff went to Moscow to ask the dramatist's permission. Ostrovsky received him "very amiably," presented him with a copy of the drama and told him to use it as he saw fit.

Rimsky-Korsakoff took his family—now consisting of wife and three children—to the country, where he set to work at *The Snow-Maiden.* No previous composition, he said, had ever come to him with such ease and rapidity. He began the Prologue on June 13, and finished the closing chorus on August 24.

The Snow-Maiden did not live up to its composer's hopes. For its première, on February 10, 1882, numerous cuts were made in the score, at each of which the composer bled. "What was to be done? One had to grin and bear it." Forty-minute intermissions dragged the opera out until nearly midnight. Reviews were hostile, with Cui, as usual, leading the attack. The *Koochka* was indeed extinct. But, just as a new circle had grown up around Balakirev, another had begun to orbit about Rimsky-Korsakoff. It included three composers who had been his pupils: Anatole Liadov, M. M. Ippolitov-Ivanov ("Caucasian Sketches"), and the precocious sixteen-year-old Alexander Glazunov, who had already heard his First Symphony performed.

Balakirev occasionally dropped in at Rimsky-Korsakoff's home, and left early. "After his departure, everyone breathed more freely."

In 1883, following the assassination of Tsar Alexander II and the accession to the throne of Alexander III, Rimsky-Korsakoff exchanged his bandmaster's post for that of assistant to Balakirev at the Court Chapel.

Musically, Rimsky-Korsakoff found the Chapel splendid, running on well-established lines going back sixty years to Bortniansky's time. He was touched, however, by the plight of the illiterate choirboys, "beaten without mercy, uneducated, taught the violin, piano or 'cello only after a fashion, ignorant and unaccustomed to work—they as a rule met with a sorry fate after the loss of their voices. From their ranks came scriveners, common servants, provincial singers, drunkards, and—at best—ignorant precentors and petty officials."

Rimsky-Korsakoff took the matter in hand, and after several seasons could note with satisfaction that illiterate choirboys were a thing of the past.

Several unproductive years now followed. Rimsky-Korsakoff felt that with *The Snow-Maiden* he had written a full stop to his career. In his head there was "only the Toricellian vacuum." He predicted that with his Chapel duties, "and with Balakirev to boot," all ambition would disappear.

In the summer of 1887, creativity returned. He had been putting *Prince Igor* in order and working halfheartedly at a display-piece for solo violin and orchestra based on Spanish themes. Suddenly Rimsky-Korsakoff was struck by inspiration: He would write a display-piece not for solo violin but for the whole orchestra. *Prince Igor* had to wait while Rimsky-Korsakoff composed the "Capriccio Espagnol."

Rimsky-Korsakoff had calculated on writing a brilliant showpiece, and his calculation was correct. At its first rehearsal it received an accolade; when the opening movement was finished the whole orchestra began to applaud. Similar applause followed the other sections. With the "Capriccio" Rimsky-Korsakoff established himself as one of the greatest orchestral technicians of his century. The next year he re-asserted his mastery with the equally brilliant "Scheherazade," and the showy "Russian Easter" Overture. The onetime duffer at instrumentation had come a long way.

In 1890, Rimsky-Korsakoff scored a personal triumph by conducting a concert of Russian music in Brussels. Otherwise the year was an unhappy one. His eighty-eight-year-old mother died; soon thereafter the Rimsky-Korsakoffs lost their youngest child, Slavchik. Rimsky-Korsakoff's new opera, *Mlada*, did not please him; nor, later on, did it please the public.

Rimsky-Korsakoff was tired of music. One morning he found himself "overtaken by an extreme lassitude accompanied by a sort of rush to my head and utter confusion of thinking." (Perhaps a mild cerebral stroke.) Frightened, he gave up working altogether. He toyed with the idea of writing a book on aesthetics, of studying philosophy, of moving from St. Petersburg to Moscow. There was a fresh personal grief, the death of his little daughter Masha.

On the death of Tchaikovsky in 1893, Rimsky-Korsakoff was asked to lead a memorial concert of Tchaikovsky's works. The concert was so successful that Rimsky-Korsakoff conducted all the Russian Musical Society concerts of the following season.

Conducting roused him from his lethargy, and reminded him of a half-forgotten project, that of turning his early symphonic poem based on the legend of Sadko, the minstrel, into an opera.

Everything, seemingly, went wrong with *Sadko*. While writing it, Rimsky-Korsakoff was frequently overcome by fatigue. He spent more than a year in completing the score. When he auditioned it before the Directorate of Theatres his pupil Felix Blumenfeld was out of sorts and played carelessly; the composer, who was singing, was nervous and soon grew hoarse. The opera was not performed to the end "owing to the lateness of the hour." Rimsky-Korsakoff resolved "never to trouble the Directorate again" with an opera score.

He offered *Sadko* to a private opera company in Moscow, which performed it on January 8, 1898. It was a hasty, badly-rehearsed performance. At one point there was an awkward stage-wait while scenery was shifted. The orchestral parts, as they had been copied, were full of errors and several instruments were missing. In one scene the chorus sang from music "held in their hands like a restaurant menu"; in another scene they did not sing at all.

Nevertheless *Sadko* took the public by storm. It

was Rimsky-Korsakoff's first opera to have an instant, unquestionable triumph. The now-hackneyed "Song of India," Sadko's duet with the Sea Princess, and other famous passages made their effect, and the exasperated composer was deluged with laurel wreaths and curtain-calls.

Later the opera had a more finished performance in St. Petersburg, with the composer conducting, and established for itself a secure place in the repertory.

This was exactly the encouragement Rimsky-Korsakoff needed. The history of his next few years is little more than a catalogue of his compositions. Besides songs and chamber music, he wrote a one-act opera, *Mozart and Salieri*, and the full-length operas *Servilia*, *The Tsar's Bride*, *Pan Veyovoda*, *The Invisible City of Kitezh*.

While Rimsky-Korsakoff was finishing *Kitezh*, Russian troops were dying at Port Arthur. The defeat in the Russo-Japanese War of immense Russia by tiny Japan was a humiliating disaster. The revolutionary ferment in St. Petersburg increased. By January, 1905, the city was virtually in a state of siege.

Students, as always happens, took part in the demonstrations, including students from the conservatory. It was proposed to expel the student ringleaders, to bring a police patrol into the school, or to close it entirely. When Rimsky-Korsakoff defended the students, he was regarded "almost as the leader of the revolutionary movement among them."

Rimsky-Korsakoff was dismissed, along with more than a hundred students, and the conservatory was closed. At once Rimsky-Korsakoff found himself the martyr-hero of the revolutionary movement. From organizations all over Russia he received deputations, letters and addresses of sympathy.

Defiantly, Rimsky-Korsakoff orchestrated "Dubinushka," one of the popular revolutionary songs of the period; then went to the country and morosely set to work at writing his memoirs.

These ended on a gloomy note. Since finishing *Kitezh*, wrote Rimsky-Korsakoff, he had been asking himself "whether it was not high time to write finis to my career as composer. . . . I had no desire to get into the stupid position of 'a singer who had lost his voice.' . . . Well, we shall see."

The memoirs were dated September 4, 1906. Just six weeks later, Rimsky-Korsakoff jotted down in his notebook the cockcrow theme of *Le Coq d'Or*.

A little more than a year later, on September 11, 1907, the score was finished. When it was submitted for performance, the composer once more found himself in trouble with the authorities. In the days of the Romanoffs, monarchy was a topic to be treated reverently, if at all. The Imperial censorship frowned on mere portrayal of royalty on the stage. *Le Coq d'Or*, with its King Dodon depicted as a dull-witted fellow outsmarted at every turn, made the censor's blood-pressure shoot up several degrees.

Ultimately *Le Coq d'Or* survived censorship and revolution to make a triumphant tour of the world's opera houses, becoming a special favorite at the

Metropolitan Opera in New York. Rimsky-Korsakoff did not live to see it performed anywhere, dying after a brief illness on June 21, 1908.

CAPRICCIO ESPAGNOL, OP. 34

Rimsky-Korsakoff, the onetime duffer who orchestrated by guesswork and corrected his scoring errors at the first rehearsal, had by 1887 become a consummate orchestral technician. Few works put an orchestra so on its mettle as the "Capriccio Espagnol," or give it a better opportunity to show what it can do. Hearing this brilliant, fiery work, one does not wonder that the musicians themselves cheered it at its first rehearsal.

So many genuinely first-rate performances of this work are available on disks that there seems no point in including versions which are musically inferior, poorly engineered or obsolete as recorded sound.

An outstanding performance is led by Eugene Ormandy. For its combination of musically sound performance, individual virtuosity of orchestra players and well-recorded sound, Ormandy's recording with the Philadelphia Orchestra can hardly be surpassed.

Fine musicianship also characterizes the lucid, well-balanced performance under Ansermet. Galliera's performance is sparkling, and Rossi's has power and intensity. Agenta's recording is one of the superior ones, and Fiedler's is not to be overlooked, either as performance or as recorded sound.

Scherchen's version shows a keen sense of drama, though tending at times toward the extremes so beautifully avoided by Ansermet. Paray's performance is at a high level of competence, as are those of Fournet and Désormière.

—Philadelphia Orchestra, Eugene Ormandy, cond. COLUMBIA CL-707 (with Tchaikovsky: *Capriccio Italien*)

—Orchestre de la Suisse Romande, Ernest Ansermet, cond. LONDON LL-1000 (with Glazounov: *Stenka Razin*)

—Philharmonia Orchestra, Alceo Galliera, cond. ANGEL 35346 (with Borodin: *Symphony No. 1*)

—Vienna State Opera Orchestra, Mario Rossi, cond. VANGUARD 484 (with *"Russian Easter" Overture*; Tchaikovsky: *Capriccio Italien*; *"1812" Overture*)

—London Symphony Orchestra, Ataulfo Argenta, cond. LONDON LL-1682 (with Chabrier: *España*; Moszkowski: *Spanish Dances*)

—Boston Pops Orchestra, Arthur Fiedler, cond. RCA VICTOR LM-9027 (with Chopin: *Les Sylphides*; Mendelssohn: *"Fingal's Cave" Overture*; Tchaikovsky: *Marche Slave*)

—London Symphony Orchestra, Hermann Scherchen, cond. WESTMINSTER XWN-18598 (with Tchaikovsky: *Capriccio Italien*; Rossini: *Overtures*)

—Detroit Symphony Orchestra, Paul Paray, cond. MERCURY 50020 (with Ravel: *Bolero*)

—Detroit Symphony Orchestra, Paul Paray, cond. MERCURY 50039 (with: *"Russian Easter" Overture*)

—Lamoureux Orchestra, Jean Fournet, cond. EPIC

LC-3432 (with Borodin: *In the Steppes*; Mussorgsky: *A Night on Bald Mountain*; Glinka: *Kamarinskaya*)

—French National Symphony, Roger Désormière, cond. CAPITOL P-8155 (with Rimsky-Korsakoff: *"Coq d'Or" Suite*)

"CHRISTMAS EVE" SUITE

Rimsky-Korsakoff had long been drawn to Gogol's *Christmas Eve* as an opera subject. Tchaikovsky had tried it, and, in Rimsky-Korsakoff's opinion, had sevened out. While his colleague was living, Rimsky-Korsakoff would not dream of hurting his feelings by setting the same work to music. The death of Tchaikovsky, however, he felt had "released" the story. In 1894 he began to set it to music.

Christmas Eve encountered difficulty from the start. For one thing, even though *Sadko* and *Coq d'Or* were still to come, Rimsky-Korsakoff was temporarily in a slump. He knew it, and his friends knew it. A good deal of the *Christmas Eve* music was manufactured rather than inspired.

Rehearsals went badly. Feodor Chaliapin, who sang a minor role, recalled how Rimsky-Korsakoff, wearing a black frock coat years out of style and trousers with old-fashioned horizontal pockets, with two pairs of spectacles on his nose, advanced reasons why the opera should not be cut; while Napravnik, speaking coldly, methodically, with a Czech accent, pointed out why it should.

There were troubles with the censor, resolved by changing Catherine the Great to a baritone. Nevertheless the Imperial family showed its displeasure by staying away from the première. Rimsky-Korsakoff showed *his* displeasure by staying away too.

An opera with sufficient vitality might have triumphed over official displeasure, as did *Rigoletto* and *Un Ballo in Maschera.* The fatal flaw of *Christmas Eve* was well described by the composer himself:

"Having read and re-read in Afanasyev about the connection between the Christian celebration of Christmas and the birth of the sun after the winter solstice, etc., I conceived the idea of introducing these extinct beliefs into the Ukrainian life described by Gogol. In this way my libretto contained much extraneous matter dragged in by me. To me and to those who desired to delve into it and understand me, this connection was clear; but to audiences, subsequently, it proved incomprehensible and even disturbing."

The inevitable consequence was that *Christmas Eve* was, operatically speaking, not long for this world. The surviving orchestral suite receives knowledgeable and affectionate treatment from Ansermet.

—Orchestre de la Suisse Romande, Ernest Ansermet, cond. LONDON LL-1733 (with: *"Sadko" Suite; Flight of the Bumblebee; Dubinushka*)

CONCERTO, IN C-SHARP MINOR, FOR PIANO, OP. 30
Among his works produced during the season of 1881-82, Rimsky-Korsakoff noted, was "a Piano Concerto in C-sharp Minor on a Russian theme,

chosen not without Balakirev's advice. In all ways
the concerto proved a chip from Liszt's concertos.
It must be said that it sounded beautiful and proved
entirely satisfactory in the sense of piano technique
and style; this greatly astonished Balakirev, who
found my concerto to his liking. He had by no
means expected that I, who was not a pianist, should
know how to compose anything entirely pianistic."

Despite the composer's high opinion of the work,
it has not become a fixture in the repertory. Pianists
do not find it rewarding enough to take the trouble
to learn it. Thanks to its availability on disks, however, one can see how Rimsky-Korsakoff made out
in trying his hand at an unfamiliar idiom. The
excellent performance by Badura-Skoda is the preferred version.

—Paul Badura-Skoda, pianist; London Philharmonic Symphony Orchestra, Artur Rodzinski,
  cond. WESTMINSTER XWN-18521 (with Franck:
  Symphonic Variations; Scriabin: *Concerto in F-
  sharp Minor*)
—Fabienne Jacquinot, pianist; Philharmonia Orchestra, Anatole Fistoulari, cond. MGM 3045
  (with *Orchestral program, Fistoulari, George Weldon, Walter Susskind, conds.*)

LE COQ D'OR—OPERA AND SUITE
This ancient tale is of Eastern origin; a slightly
different version brought by the Moors to Spain
is told by Washington Irving in *The Alhambra*.

Le Coq d'Or involved Rimsky-Korsakoff in fresh
trouble with the authorities—and small wonder,
since comically inept King Dodon is an obvious dig

at bumbling, fumbling officialdom. On this point, as Boris Pasternak's experience with *Doctor Zhivago* shows, commissars are as touchy as Imperial censors.

Somewhat curiously, in view of the number of obscure and seldom-performed operas which have found their way into the record repertory, there is no complete *Coq d'Or* in the catalogue.

The opera itself is no stranger to the world's opera houses. Its first U. S. performance took place at the Metropolitan Opera on March 6, 1917, with a double cast of singers who performed from the orchestra pit and dancers who mimed the action on stage. The difficult, brilliant coloratura role of the Queen was sung by Maria Barrientos, with Adamo Didur as King Dodon. Other coloraturas heard in the role of the Queen included Mabel Garrison, Amelita Galli-Curci and Marion Talley.

The dual-cast arrangement remained in effect until 1936, when *Le Coq d'Or* was both sung and acted by a cast headed by Lily Pons and Ezio Pinza.

Le Coq d'Or, shot through with the vivid exoticism which Rimsky-Korsakoff used with such telling effect, makes a stunning impression in the theatre. Perhaps it will be available on disks in the future. Meanwhile the orchestral suite from the opera sketched by the composer shortly before his death is available in a number of excellent performances.

The performance under Golovanov is a spirited one. Ansermet's exhibits the polish and refinement typical of the Genevans. Fiedler's offers the well-recorded sound of a fine orchestra. Generally capable performances are those under Dobrowen, Désormière and Dorati.

—USSR State Radio Orchestra, Nikolai Golovanov, cond. VANGUARD 6000 (with Mussorgsky: A *Night on Bald Mountain*)

—Orchestre de la Suisse Romande, Ernest Ansermet, cond. LONDON LL-694 (with: *Capriccio Espagnol*)

—Boston Pops Orchestra, Arthur Fiedler, cond. RCA VICTOR LM-2100 (with Rossini: "*William Tell*" *Overture*; Tchaikovsky: *Marche Slave*)

—Philharmonia Orchestra, Issay Dobrowen, cond. ANGEL 35010 (with "*Tsar Saltan*" *Suite*)

—French National Symphony Orchestra, Roger Désormière, cond. CAPITOL P-8155 (with: *Capriccio Espagnol*)

—London Symphony Orchestra, Antal Dorati, cond. MERCURY 50122 (with Borodin: *Polovtsian Dances*)

DUBINUSHKA

This orchestral setting of a stirring revolutionary song was a by-product of Rimsky-Korsakoff's participation in the political uproar of 1905. Having been dismissed from his conservatory post, Rimsky-Korsakoff defiantly made a short orchestra piece of "Dubinushka." As punishment the public performance of his music was forbidden. Two months later the authorities relented and still later the composer was re-instated in his professorship.

The spirited work is heard in a fine performance by Ansermet and the Geneva forces.

—Orchestre de la Suisse Romande, Ernest Ansermet, cond. LONDON LL-1733 (with *Flight of the*

Bumblebee; "Christmas Eve" Suite; "Sadko" Suite)

FANTASY ON RUSSIAN THEMES, OP. 33

In 1886, Rimsky-Korsakoff, having become interested in violin technique as a result of his instrumental class at the Imperial Chapel, conceived the idea of writing a display-piece for violin and orchestra, on Russian themes. He tried it out with his orchestra of chapel pupils, and was so pleased with the result that he determined to compose another, on Spanish themes. As already noted, this was finally metamorphosed into the brilliant "Capriccio Espagnol."

The available recording of the "Fantasy on Russian Themes" is noteworthy for the fine playing of a Soviet violinist, Marina Kozulupova.

—Marina Kozulupova, violinist; USSR State Radio Orchestra, Samuel Anasov, cond. WESTMINSTER XWN-18120 (with *Sadko excerpts;* Balakirev: *Russia)*

"IVAN THE TERRIBLE" SUITE

The opera, Ivan the Terrible, also known as *Pskovityanka (The Maid of Pskov)*, was Rimsky-Korsakoff's first. When it was premièred in 1873, the conductor, Napravnik, suggested a number of changes. "Youth," said the composer in later years, "made me fly into a passion; I therefore yielded nothing."

With the perspective of time and experience, Rimsky-Korsakoff saw that Napravnik had been, by and large, right. He therefore revised the opera completely in 1875, and made a second revision two years later.

Nevertheless, even as revised, the opera, now generally known as *Ivan the Terrible*, has not held the stage. The orchestral suite drawn from the score receives deft and sympathetic treatment from Fistoulari.

—London Symphony Orchestra, Anatole Fistoulari, cond. MGM E-3076 (with Balakirev: *Tamar*)

"Legend of the Invisible City of Kitezh" Suite

This opera, another in Rimsky-Korsakoff's long series of works based on fantastic or supernatural themes, was completed in rough draft during the summer of 1903. It was after finishing *Kitezh* that the composer asked himself whether he ought not, finally, to give up composing.

At its first performance, in February, 1907, *Kitezh* had a mixed reception. One critic recommended combining Acts III and IV into one, and leaving out Act II entirely. By then, the sixty-three-year-old composer was too deep in writing *Coq d'Or* to mind.

The orchestral suite made from *Kitezh*, a rarity seldom heard in concert-hall performance, in this country at least, is played with spirit under Graunke's direction.

—Bavarian Symphony Orchestra, Kurt Graunke, cond. Urania URLP-7115 (with *"Russian Easter"* *Overture*; d'Indy: *Istar*)

May Night

May Night, begun in the summer of 1878, is based on a story by Gogol. It was the type of subject which invariably fascinated Rimsky-Korsakoff, combining elements of folk pageantry, the supernatural and the ancient pagan sun-worship of pre-Christian Russia.

Its chief distinction is the sheer beauty of the music. A *May Night* was once lent to a staff member of the Metropolitan Opera, who was so taken by it that for a time it appeared legal action would be necessary to get the recording back.

J. J. Fux, great contrapuntalist whose *Gradus ad Parnassum* of 1725 is still authoritative, advised composers to submit to the dry and seemingly pointless drudgery of counterpoint on somewhat the same principle as Glenn Cunningham's running the mile in lumberjack's boots. When their fetters were released, so to speak, said Fux, they would find "to their surprise and delight" that they could write free composition as if it were play.

It was in *May Night* that Rimsky-Korsakoff, as he put it, "cast off the shackles of counterpoint." The laborious discipline to which he had subjected himself had been fully assimilated. Thereafter he was able to write with complete ease and spontaneity.

"May Night," said the composer, was "bound up in my mind with memories of the time when my wife became my fiancée." The opera is dedicated to her.

—Soloists, chorus and orchestra of the Bolshoi Theatre, Vassily Nebolsin, cond. Three 12-in. VANGUARD VRS-6006/8

MOZART AND SALIERI, OP. 48

A musical legend which absolutely refuses to die is that Mozart was poisoned. Cited as supporting evidence are the suddenness of the seizure which proved fatal; the violence of the composer's death-throes; and the haste and secrecy with which his body was disposed of in a grave which has never been found.

One version of the legend is that Mozart, a member of the New-Crowned Hope Lodge of Vienna, had in *The Magic Flute* made disclosures of Masonic ritual which the brotherhood considered indiscreet, and accordingly received "the mysterious *aqua toffana* which has dispatched unworthy Masons to the Beyond since earliest times." A further embellishment is that the mysterious black-clad stranger who appeared out of nowhere to commission the Requiem was in reality an emissary of the Lodge, and that the gloom known to have pervaded Mozart's last days was caused by the realization that his number was up.

A variant of this legend is that the poison was administered by the Austro-Italian composer Antonio Salieri (Schubert's teacher), who was unable to endure the contrast between the perfection of Mozart's music and the imperfection of his own.

Pushkin's play based on the Salieri variant of "Who Struck Mozart?" was turned into a one-act opera by Rimsky-Korsakoff. Excerpts from Mozart's own works are quoted, and at other points Rimsky-Korsakoff rather prided himself on the skill with which he had written music in Mozartean style. Although the opera is now out of the catalogue, a little browsing among record dealers might turn up one of the two extant recordings. The Bolshoi performance in Russian is preferable to the French version conducted by Leibowitz.

—Soloists and orchestra of the Bolshoi Theatre, Samuel Samosud, cond. COLOSSEUM 10420

—Jean Mollien, tenor; Jacques Linsolas, baritone; French Radio Orchestra, René Leibowitz, cond. OCEANIC OCS-32

PROCESSION OF NOBLES, FROM "MLADA"

In the summer of 1891, Rimsky-Korsakoff suffered what appears to have been a mild cerebral stroke. He feared he had "written himself out," and was further harassed by his strained relations with Balakirev at the Imperial Chapel.

Under these circumstances, work on his opera *Mlada* went slowly. Rimsky-Korsakoff, who usually had an author's high opinion of his own work, observed that "Mlada is as cold as ice. Now a Beethoven quartet or symphony is another matter. Technique and working-out are there only the outward form, and everything is filled with life and soul. I fancy that a great part of the Russian school is not music, but cold, brain-spun stuff. Having such thoughts, I ought to leave off composing."

Mlada bore out the composer's gloomy prediction. After a brilliantly successful first performance in November, 1892, the opera gradually disappeared from the repertory. It is kept alive by the impressive "Procession of Nobles," which appears regularly on concert programs. Weldon leads the London Symphony in a capable performance of the work.

—London Symphony Orchestra, George Weldon, cond. MGM 3045 (with: *Orchestral program, Weldon, Anatole Fistoulari and Walter Susskind, conds.*)

QUINTET, IN B-FLAT, FOR PIANO AND WINDS

Rimsky-Korsakoff wrote this piece in 1876 for a prize competition sponsored by the Russian Musical Society. The prize went to a trio by the conductor-composer Napravnik.

Rimsky-Korsakoff's version of the affair was that the Napravnik trio had a superb pianist in the great Theodor Leschetizky; whereas a poor sight reader named Cross had made such a hash of his quintet that the jury did not hear it to the end. But, said Rimsky-Korsakoff, his quintet "pleased the public greatly" when subsequently performed.

A further tidbit added by Rimsky-Korsakoff was that the Grand Duke Constantine told him, after making the award: "What a pity we did not know the work was thine" (using the intimate form of speech).

Perhaps Rimsky-Korsakoff was unjustly deprived of first prize; the Napravnik trio has certainly vanished without a trace.

But it was fortunate for Rimsky-Korsakoff that his reputation did not depend on the quintet alone. It is a transitional work, written while Rimsky-Korsakoff was still a stiff and self-conscious contrapuntalist. He had not yet entirely "cast off the shackles of counterpoint." The quintet is learned, labored, ingenious and rather dry.

For what it is worth, it is earnestly performed by the Viennese players.

—Roland Raupenstrauch, pianist; Vienna Philharmonic Wind Group. WESTMINSTER XWN-18071 (with: *Sinfonietta*)

"RUSSIAN EASTER" OVERTURE

In the summer of 1888, Rimsky-Korsakoff wrote the two compositions which are standard in the repertory of every orchestra—"Scheherazade" and the "Russian Easter" Overture.

"In order to appreciate my Overture even ever so slightly," wrote Rimsky-Korsakoff, "it is necessary for the hearer to have attended Easter morning service at least once, and not in a domestic chapel, but in a cathedral thronged with people from every walk of life, with several priests conducting the cathedral service—something that many intellectual Russian hearers, let alone hearers of other confessions, quite lack nowadays."

In his autograph score, Rimsky-Korsakoff quoted the opening of Psalm LXVIII: "Let God arise, let his enemies be scattered; let them also that hate him flee before him." The slow, rather lengthy introduction is based on the theme of "Let God arise" as used in the Russian Orthodox service. Interwoven with it is another ecclesiastical theme, associated with the prophecy of Isaiah.

The "gloomy colors of the Andante lugubre," Rimsky-Korsakoff tells us, depict the Holy Sepulchre. A transition leads to the Allegro, the Resurrection narrative as told in Mark XVI. Finally another canticle of the Orthodox service, "Christ is Risen," sounds amid trumpet fanfares and the pealing of bells.

For all its Orthodoxy, the "Russian Easter" Overture is a superb opportunity for an orchestra to show what it can do. Ansermet's interpretations is a brilliant piece of orchestral playing, not wasted by the London engineers. Scherchen's abounds in dramatic contrasts, and shows a strong feeling for orchestral color. Paray's has less dramatic emphasis, and is somewhat less brightly recorded.

The Stokowski performance glows with opulent orchestral tone color and is musically individualistic. Rossi's has the bright colors, minus the mannerisms. The Fiedler, Boult and Graunke performances are straightforward, musicianly but not particularly striking interpretations.

—Orchestre de la Suisse Romande, Ernest Ansermet, cond. LONDON LL-1635 (with *"May Night" Overture; "Tsar Saltan" Suite*)

—London Symphony Orchestra, Hermann Scherchen, cond. WESTMINSTER XWN-18282 (with *Symphony No. 2*)

—Detroit Symphony Orchestra, Paul Paray, cond. MERCURY 50028 (with *Symphony No. 2*)

—Leopold Stokowski and his Symphony Orchestra. RCA VICTOR LM-1816 (with Mussorgsky: *A Night on Bald Mountain; "Khovantschina" excerpts*; Borodin: *In the Steppes*)

—Vienna State Opera Orchestra, Mario Rossi, cond. VANGUARD 484 (with *Capriccio Espagnol*; Tchaikovsky: *"1812" Overture; Capriccio Italien*)

—Boston Pops Orchestra, Arthur Fiedler, cond. RCA VICTOR LM-2202 (with Borodin: *"Prince Igor" excerpts; In the Steppes*)

—London Philharmonic Orchestra, Sir Adrian Boult, cond. RCA VICTOR LM-2185 (with Rachmaninoff: *Symphony No. 3*)

—Bavarian Symphony Orchestra, Kurt Graunke, cond. URANIA URLP-7115 (with *"Kitezh" Suite*; d'Indy: *Istar*)

SADKO

The story of Sadko, the Minstrel, and his adventures under the sea was an ancient Russian legend which delighted Rimsky-Korsakoff. He set it to music in an opera which, although it exhibits the Russian national trait of discursiveness, in its best moments is a delight.

Everyone exposed to Music by Muzak knows the "Song of India" from *Sadko*. Less familiar, and worth hearing, is the enchanting love duet between Sadko and the Sea Princess. Another highlight is the sprightly Chorus of the Merchants of Nizhi-Novgorod, which has the odd signature of 11/8 time.

Efrem Zimbalist, who was Rimsky-Korsakoff's pupil at the conservatory and took part in the 1905 student demonstration which got the composer into hot water with the authorities, recalls, of a turn-of-the-century *Sadko* performance, that the 11/8 chorus perplexed the conductor. How should he beat it? In other words, should it be subdivided into groups of four, four and three; three, three, three and two; five and six?

It occurred to somebody that Rimsky-Korsakoff, experienced bandmaster, was just the man to settle the question.

Rimsky-Korsakoff, says Mr. Zimbalist, studied the score, thoughtfully stroking his beard; then counted out the Russian equivalent of:

"ONE-two-three-four; FIVE-six-seven-eight; NINE-ten-ele-VEN."

Sadko is another Rimsky-Korsakoff opera which is, unfortunately, out of the catalogue. It is worth while to go to a little trouble to turn up a copy in the second-hand market.

—Soloists, chorus, orchestra and stage band of the Bolshoi Theatre, Nikolai Golovanov, cond. Three 12-in. CONCERT HALL SOCIETY CHS-1307

SCHEHERAZADE

No work of Rimsky-Korsakoff is better known, or more frequently played, than this musical treatment of episodes from the *Thousand and One Nights*. First heard in 1888, it quickly made its way around the world and has been a concert-hall standby ever since.

Of the many excellent recordings available, especially colorful is Stokowski's with the Philharmonia Orchestra. Mario Rossi also achieves brilliant results with the Vienna State Opera Orchestra. And the Beecham reading is spirited, with the special quality of enthusiasm which Sir Thomas is able to evoke from an orchestra.

Ansermet's recording is not sensational in any way, but everything which can be said about it is good: It is a musicianly performance, recorded with exceptional clarity and brightness.

Ormandy's performance is superlative recorded sound, but the effects sound a little too calculated. Everything is planned for effect. It is a fine example of the art of record-making, if not of musical performance.

Steinberg's is a musicianly, capable performance, with vividly-recorded orchestral sound. Dorati's is a brilliant recording of a somewhat commonplace performance. Fricsay's sounds carefully rehearsed and carefully recorded, to the extent that the spontaneity and freshness which this music needs are lacking. And despite Van Beinum's erudition and fine musicianship, his performance to some extent suffers from the same fault.

Capable, unspectacular readings are those of Monteux, Dobrowen, Perlea and Scherchen.

—Philharmonia Orchestra, Leopold Stokowski, cond. RCA Victor lm-1732

—Vienna State Opera Orchestra, Mario Rossi, cond. Vanguard srv-103

—Royal Philharmonic Orchestra, Sir Thomas Beecham, cond. Angel 35505

—Paris Conservatory Orchestra, Ernest Ansermet, cond. London ll-1162

—Philadelphia Orchestra, Eugene Ormandy, cond. Columbia cl-850

—Pittsburgh Symphony Orchestra, William Steinberg, cond. Capitol p-8305

—Minneapolis Symphony Orchestra, Antal Dorati, cond. Mercury 50009

—Berlin Radio Symphony Orchestra, Ferenc Fricsay, cond. Decca 9908

—Amsterdam Concertgebouw Orchestra, Eduard van Beinum, cond. Epic lc-3300

—London Symphony Orchestra, Pierre Monteux, cond. RCA Victor lm-2208

—Philharmonia Orchestra, Issay Dobrowen, cond. Angel 35009

—Bamberg Symphony Orchestra, Jonel Perlea, cond.
Vox 10220

—Vienna State Opera Orchestra, Hermann Scherchen, cond. WESTMINSTER XWN-18660

SINFONIETTA ON RUSSIAN THEMES

In the summer of 1879, Rimsky-Korsakoff composed a string quartet, which he asked the Davydov
Quartet to play over for him. The players did not
think much of it; nor did the composer. "The first
movement was monotonous; the Scherzo had no
coda; and the Finale was dry. I did not venture to
let the public hear my quartet."

Instead, the following year, as a diversion from
his labors on *The Snow-Maiden*, Rimsky-Korsakoff
recast the quartet as a sinfonietta. He overhauled
the first three movements and threw out the "dry"
finale entirely.

This pleasant work, abounding in characteristic
Rimsky-Korsakoff touches, receives sympathetic
treatment from Swoboda and the Vienna players.

—Vienna Symphony Orchestra, Henry Swoboda,
cond. WESTMINSTER XWN-18071 (with: *Quintet
in B-flat*)

SKAZKA, OP. 29

"Skazka" ("Fairy-Tale") was composed at the same
time (1880-81) as *The Snow-Maiden*, and strongly
resembles it in style. It was suggested by the fairy-
tale episodes jotted down by Pushkin in his Prologue to *Russlan and Ludmilla*. Rimsky-Korsakoff,
however, was vexed when listeners supposed he
had followed Pushkin literally. "I narrate my own

musical fairy-tale," he tells us. "Let everyone seek in my fairy-tale only the episodes that may appear before his imagination, but let him not insist that I include everything enumerated in Pushkin's prologue."

The pleasant, colorful work is heard in lively and imaginative performance under Fistoulari's direction.

—Philharmonia Orchestra, Anatole Fistoulari, cond. MGM 3017 (with *"Snow-Maiden" Suite*)

THE SNOW-MAIDEN

In his later years, Rimsky-Korsakoff devoted himself principally to opera. One type of subject attracted him especially—a humorous or fantastic tale folklike in character, with pantheistic elements such as the sun-cult of pre-Christian Slavic paganism.

Such a work was Ostrovsky's *The Snow-Maiden*, which Rimsky-Korsakoff set just in time to prevent Tchaikovsky from doing so, to the latter's great annoyance.

Essentially *The Snow-Maiden* is a wintry Northern version of the legend of Proserpina. The heroine, instead of being kept underground, is turned to ice; the touch of the sun's rays would be fatal.

A perennially fascinating speculation is whether Ostrovsky consciously borrowed from the Greek legend, or whether the tale, on which the play was based, had a more ancient folk origin. Might it even have come up from the South, when the armies of Alexander the Great reached the banks of the River Oxus?

The folklorist Afanasyev appears to have believed this a possibility.

Whatever its origin, the drama fascinated Rimsky-Korsakoff. In the summer of 1880 he took his family to the country and set to work on *The Snow-Maiden*. Ideas came to him faster than he could write them down, he tells us. He sat down to compose the Prologue on June 1, and finished the four-act, six-hundred-page opera on August 12.

Steeped in the sights and sounds of a Russian village, Rimsky-Korsakoff strove to evoke in his score a feeling of folk idiom, placing special emphasis on the Dorian, Phrygian and Mixolydian modes. So successful was he in this that the critic M. M. Ivanov charged that Rimsky-Korsakoff had filled his score from end to end with folk tunes because he was unable to invent melodies of his own.

Enraged, Rimsky-Korsakoff in a letter to the editor invited the critic to identify the folk tunes. "Of course," he added, "no such statement was forthcoming."

After the usual pulling and hauling incidental to the production of any new opera, *The Snow-Maiden* was performed at St. Petersburg in January, 1882. The role of King Frost was sung by F. I. Stravinsky, father of the composer, Igor Stravinsky. The opera was a success and gradually made its way to all the great opera houses of the world, including the Metropolitan.

An excellent recording by the Belgrade National Opera is available.

—Soloists, chorus and orchestra of the Belgrade National Opera, Kreshimir Baranovich, cond. Five 12-in. LONDON XLLA-45

SYMPHONY No. 2, OP. 9 ("ANTAR")

This youthful work was written in the summer of 1868 while Rimsky-Korsakoff was staying in the apartment of his brother Voin, who was away on a practice cruise. The composer was to revise "Antar" three times thereafter, never getting it entirely to his satisfaction.

Looking back with the perspective of thirty years, Rimsky-Korsakoff thought that "Antar" had come off fairly well, considering his abysmal ignorance of the composer's craft. "Still, I was wrong in calling 'Antar' a symphony. It was a poem, suite, fairy-tale, story, or anything you like, but not a symphony. Its structure in four separate movements was all that made it approach a symphony. It has no thematic development whatever—only variations and paraphrases."

Later on, the composer rechristened it a "symphonic suite." By whatever name, it is minor Rimsky-Korsakoff.

Ansermet's fine musicianship and flawless sense of proportion makes the work sound, on the whole, somewhat better than it is. Paray's performance is thoughtful and sensitive; Scherchen's tends to dramatize, and sometimes overdramatize, the music.

—Orchestre de la Suisse Romande, Ernest Ansermet, cond. LONDON LL-1060 (with Glazounov: *Stenka Razin*)

—Detroit Symphony Orchestra, Paul Paray, cond. MERCURY 50028 (with *"Russian Easter" Overture*)

—London Symphony Orchestra, Hermann Scherchen, cond. WESTMINSTER xwn-18282 (with *"Russian Easter" Overture*)

SYMPHONY No. 3 IN C

In 1873 the ignorant conservatory professor, crammed with still-undigested lumps of Bellermann on counterpoint, Tchaikovsky on harmony, and Berlioz on instrumentation, sat down to write another symphony.

"Work on the first movement of the symphony was slow," he recalled, "and beset with difficulties. I strove to crowd in as much counterpoint as possible; but being unskilled in it and hard put to combine the themes and motives, I drained my immediate flow of imagination considerably. The cause of this was, of course, my insufficient technique; yet I was irresistibly drawn to add greater interest to the structural style of my compositions."

Rimsky-Korsakoff's earnestness and sincerity of purpose were so evident that Cui, reviewing the first performance, gave him E for effort: The symphony, he wrote, was "the fruit of ripe thought, happy inspiration and strong talent combined with deep and solid technical knowledge."

Others of the Five disagreed. They thought the symphony merely dull. Posterity has, on the whole, concurred.

If earnest efforts and loving attention to detail could rescue a work from quasi-oblivion, the performance by Gauk and the Bolshoi forces would do so for the Third Symphony.

—Bolshoi Symphony Orchestra, Alexander Gauk, cond. PERIOD 567 (with Glière: *Harp Concerto*)

"Tsar Saltan" Suite

Tsar Saltan, written in 1899-1900, was based on a fairy-tale of the same name by Pushkin. In the enchanted kingdom of Tsar Saltan, magic spells are an everyday affair. One of them is musically depicted in the best-known excerpt from the suite. The young Prince Gvidon, eager to see his father, Tsar Saltan, is transformed into a bumblebee to enable him to make the trip in the shortest possible time.

The complete "Tsar Saltan" Suite is given a brilliant reading by Dobrowen; a smaller-scale and more subtly shaded performance by Ansermet.

—Philharmonia Orchestra, Issay Dobrowen, cond. Angel 35010 (with *"Coq d'Or" Suite*)
—Orchestre de la Suisse Romande, Ernest Ansermet, cond. London ll-1635 (with *"May Night" Overture, "Russian Easter" Overture*)

"The Flight of the Bumblebee"

Among recordings of "The Flight of the Bumblebee," from the "Tsar Saltan" Suite, that by Ormandy and the Philadelphia Orchestra is outstanding as superb, well-recorded orchestral playing.

—Philharmonia Orchestra, Issay Dobrowen, cond. Angel 35010 (with *"Coq d'Or" Suite*)
—Orchestre de la Suisse Romande, Ernest Ansermet, cond. London ll-1635 (with *"May Night" Overture, "Russian Easter" Overture*)
—Philadelphia Orchestra, Eugene Ormandy, cond. Columbia cl-707 (with Tchaikovsky: *Capriccio Italien, Andante Cantabile*)

—Orchestre de la Suisse Romande, Ernest Ansermet, cond. LONDON LL-1733 (with *"Sadko" Suite,
"Christmas Eve" Suite; Dubinushka*)

—Hallé Orchestra, George Weldon, cond. MERCURY
50137 (with Khachaturian: *"Gayne" Ballet Suite
No. 1*; Borodin: *"Prince Igor" Overture, In the
Steppes*; Mussorgsky: A *Night on Bald Mountain*)

THE TSAR'S BRIDE

In 1898 Rimsky-Korsakoff set about a long-cherished
project, the making of an opera out of Mey's melo-
dramatic play, *The Tsar's Bride*.

His ambition was to write a genuine "singers'
opera," with arias and ensembles as formal set-
pieces. Its style was to be "cantilena par excellence," the composer wrote; it must be, above all
else, singable.

This is perhaps what Montagu-Nathan had in
mind when he wrote that the work "savors of
Mozart and the Italian opera." Aside from its purely
formal design, it is hard to find excessive "Western
influence" in this most Russian of Rimsky-Korsakoff's operas.

It was also, before the 1917 Revolution, the most
popular of his works in Russia. The Soviets apparently do not encourage Tsarism; Glinka's A *Life
for the Tsar* today goes by the title of *Ivan Susanin*.
Nevertheless, *The Tsar's Bride* is still performed at
Kiev, as the fine available recording proves.

—Soloists, chorus and orchestra of the Kiev Theatre,
Vladimir Piradov, cond. Three 12-in. WESTMIN-
STER OPW-1301.